TALENT PLANNING

Dominate your industry
with the right people and strategy

Steve Van Remortel

Copyright © 2024—by Steve Van Remortel

This book is protected by the copyright laws of the United States of America. All rights reserved. No part of this publication may be reproduced, stored in a retrieval system, or transmitted in any form or by any means, electronic or mechanical, including photocopying, recording, scanning, or otherwise, except as permitted under Section 107 or 108 of the 1967 United States Copyright Act, without the prior written permission of the author. To request permission, contact the author at **info@mytalentplanner.com**.

Driving Forces® is a registered trademark of TTI Success Insights LTD.

Mention of specific companies, organizations or authorities in this book does not imply endorsement by the author or publisher, nor does mention of specific companies, organizations, or authorities imply that they endorse this book, its author, or the publisher. All trademarks are the property of their respective companies. Internet addresses given in this book were accurate at the time it went to press.

Limit of Liability/Disclaimer of Warranty: While the author has used his best efforts in preparing this book, he makes no representations or warranties with respect to the accuracy or completeness of the contents of this book and specifically disclaims any implied warranties of merchantability or fitness for a particular purpose. No warranty may be created or extended by sales representatives or written sales materials. The author shall not be liable for any loss of profit or any other commercial damages, including but not limited to special, incidental, consequential, or other damages.

For ordering books, special discounts, bulk purchases, or information about our products or services, please visit our website at **www.mytalentplanner.com**, or contact the author at **info@mytalentplanner.com**

Manufactured in the United States of America

Contents

Maximizing This Book | v

1: Why the Hell Didn't I Plan for This? 1

2: Our Talent Deserves a Plan 11

3: Process Prep 19

4: Team Development Session 29

5: Strategy Session 41

6: Talent Vision & Sprint Goals Session 55

7: The Talent Plan for your Leadership Team 65

8: Department Plans 75

9: Meeting Cadence 83

10: Shepherd of the Talent 95

11: Develop and Dominate 103

12: The Toolkit 105

Appendix | 113

Acknowledgements | 125

About the Author | 127

Maximizing This Book

Thank you for your interest in Talent Planning! Before you begin reading about the process that will help initiate unprecedented growth in your company, as well as within your team members and yourself as a leader, I'd like to point out a few things to help you derive the utmost value from Talent Planning:

1. This is a comprehensive seven-step Talent Planning process. Each step works in concert with the next and builds off what came before it, adding up or even multiplying the incredible impact of Talent Planning. Based on leading companies through this process hundreds of times, the most effective approach to solve your people issues to accelerate growth is by completing the seven steps of the process.

2. While working through the steps reveals the full power of Talent Planning, each step can also be completed as an individual, standalone exercise. You can target a particular area of your organization that needs to be developed, solidified, or reset. For example, if you know your leadership team would benefit from improved communication, the team development exercise in Chapter 4 will work wonders and lead to breakthroughs in and of itself.

Or, if your company's vision is in place, but over time you're having trouble keeping all team members focused and accountable, you can simply flip to Chapter 9 for an effective run-through of instilling a solid meeting cadence for your organization.

3. MyTalentPlanner is the only software for executing your strategy & talent plan. The software streamlines the Talent Planning process with a single login to create your strategic vision, the talent plan to achieve it, the metrics to monitor it, the goals and action plans to make it happen, and the meeting cadence to ensure communication and accountability. MyTalentPlanner guides you through the process of solving your people issues and creating sustained acceleration of growth for your company beyond what you ever thought possible. Visit **MyTalentPlanner.com** to learn more about this unique software that helps you attract, develop, and retain talent to dominate your industry.

4. The Talent Planning process can be completed on your own, or with a talent planning advisor. With this book, and even more so with the MyTalentPlanner software, any passionate business leader has what it takes to lead his or her organization through the Talent Planning process. However, if you would rather focus on being part of the process versus leading it, especially in the first year, you can utilize the expert services of a certified talent planning advisor. Contact **info@MyTalentPlanner.com** for more information about a talent planning advisor near you.

MAXIMIZING THIS BOOK

The deeper you dive into this process, the greater your efforts will be rewarded. I am so excited for you to come on board to the future of talent—Talent Planning!

Why the Hell Didn't I Plan for This?

"A goal without a plan is just a wish."
— Antoine de Saint-Exupéry

Have you ever thought about how many plans you have in your life?

You have an investment plan. You have a health insurance plan. You have a retirement plan.

You plan for vacation—which includes who will cover for you at work while you're gone, which clothes to pack, who'll watch your house, check your mailbox, or take care of your pet while you're away.

When planning a wedding—which can sometimes feel like a part-time job—we put so much effort into it. Some of us even enlist the help of a professional wedding planner to help them plan!

We make childcare plans, meal plans, and fitness plans. Some of us make diet plans—or at least we plan to.

And that's just in our personal lives. As business owners, our efforts to grow our companies *always* involve plans, sub-plans, and planning sessions—from company strategies, to investments, marketing plans, sales plans, and so many more.

We're pretty much plan-aholics, with one painful exception: **We forget to make plans around the people in our organizations.**

What makes this blind spot so hard for us to see? Why is it so easy to overlook this obligation, even when it so drastically limits our business' growth? How many more thousands of dollars must we squander on training, re-training, and endlessly recruiting talent before we not only take notice, but take action?

My organization was bitten by people issues, repeatedly, until I eventually recognized our lack of a plan. It should have been obvious, but why wasn't it?

How could this happen? Oddly enough, this weakness can be made possible by a strength common to business leaders: resiliency. My ability to roll with unexpected punches had actually worked against me, and kept me from getting out in front of talent issues. Can you relate to that? When we're good at reacting, we can unfortunately forget to be great at planning.

But why do so many of us business leaders *really* fail to plan around our people? Candidly: because it's hard to do! We have so much on our plates, and, hey— it's not like there's a manual out there for dealing with these things.

I set about changing that. With this book, I hope to spare many of you the frustration I experienced operating under what we'll call The Old Way, meaning:

- Being reactive
- Taking a piecemeal approach, i.e., PIPs, and filling individual positions after people quit

- Hiring from the outside because there's no one to promote internally
- At most, talking about positions needed when the annual budgeting process rolls around

Why did we ever tolerate The Old Way? As business leaders, we work so hard to stay ahead of conflicts, shortages, and missteps—our every thought and action is based on putting our companies in the best possible position to succeed. So, why are we so often caught off-guard regarding our team members? *Why don't we put a plan around our people issues?*

We know The Old Way isn't acceptable—it's at odds with our otherwise proactive approach to running our businesses. Talent Planning puts us back on the offensive where we belong—heading off the people issues that, when left unaddressed, will always cap companies' growth potential. Talent Planning is your key to attracting, developing, and retaining talent to dominate your industry—The New Way you've been needing.

Strategy or Talent: Which Comes First?

In my 25plus years as a strategy and talent planning advisor, I still maintain that a business is only as good as its strategy —while recognizing an inherent paradox. Strategy is and will always need to be our company's first focus, because before we can do Talent Planning, we need to first know where we're going. *However*, a strategy is only as good as the talent in place to see it through. In other words, though strategic planning comes first, the talent plan is an organization's most important plan.

Before I started Stop the Vanilla, our strategy and talent planning advising firm, I ran a contract manufacturing food business called EnzoPac. There, with considerable hours and effort, our leadership team and I developed a *killer* differentiated strategy for our business. Our target markets just ate it up, and our eyes only widened as we pictured how our company would grow. I can't describe it any other way—it was fun!

Well, it could have been, or should have been.

Even with the perfect strategy in place to take EnzoPac to an unprecedented level of sales, we just couldn't get there. We were limited, as so many companies are, by consistent people issues.

A lingering open position in sales. Then a shocking resignation from a manager. All the while, a conflict between two team members festered, and one of our departments chronically underperformed.

Buzzkills... frustrations... judgments... man—all people issues, all tough to address, and all keeping us from hitting our stride on what should have been an endless victory lap.

We'd implemented an exciting strategic plan, an effective sales plan, and a sound financial plan—so why wasn't everything falling into place? Putting our heads together, it became clear our problems all revolved around the talent we had, or lacked, as we humbly recognized: in spite of all our planning efforts, we somehow forgot to create a plan for our talent. *Why the hell didn't I plan for this?* What a lightbulb moment.

What followed was the genesis of the Talent Planning process. We developed a three-year vision and a three-year talent plan to achieve it. Our talent plan (though we didn't call it that at the time) accelerated our growth, and EnzoPac went on the four-and-a-half-year run that we knew was in us, growing from 5 million to 30 million in sales. You can bet we used our now-sharp planning skills to plan a few celebrations!

What's at Stake: Generational Challenges

Our companies can only flourish when they're not weighed down by people issues. Talent Planning represents the future of proactively navigating and mitigating people issues by addressing them "upstream" before they materialize and negatively impact our business. At EnzoPac, it was a harsh epiphany to recognize we'd hobbled our own potential by failing to make a plan for our talent—the number one issue impacting our growth.

With the Talent Planning process—The New Way—you'll be proactive, and will no longer allow predictable, foreseeable, and internal people issues to compound the unpredictable variables and external threats that may affect your business. There's never a wise time to steer into avoidable potholes, especially as we maneuver not just an uncertain economic landscape, but certain generational challenges as well.

According to the U.S. Bureau of Labor Statistics, September 2023 saw a total of 9.61 million open jobs in America. The talent deficit in our economy has been hovering at or near record levels for several years, and generational math shows that people issues will continue to be the top issue facing organizations, above even inflation and supply chain issues.

Looking at the populations[1] of each of the four generations currently contributing to the American workforce, we

---

1. Richard Fry, "Millennials overtake Baby Boomers as America's largest generation," *Pew Research*, April 28, 2020, https://www.pewresearch.org/short-reads/2020/04/28/millennials-overtake-baby-boomers-as-americas-largest-generation/.

can better understand how we got here and where we're heading—what we refer to as generational math.

Baby Boomers: 75 million

- Born 1946-64—the oldest generation in the workforce
- 41 million are still working, comprising 25% of current talent[2]
- 39% (29 million) retired during the COVID-19 pandemic (known as "The Great Retirement")[3]
- 10,000 reach retirement age every day[4]

Generation X: 66 million

- Born 1965-80 - the second largest percentage of the workforce—33%[5]
- Contains majority of company leaders and 55% of start-up founders[6]
- Just starting to reach retirement eligibility

---

2. *Purdue Global*, "Generational Differences in the Workplace," https://www.purdueglobal.edu/education-partnerships/generational-workforce-differences-infographic/.
3. *Ibid.*
4. *Ibid.*
5. *Ibid.*
6. *Ibid.*

Millennials/Generation Y: 72 million

- Born 1981-96—highest percentage of the workforce at 35%[7], surpassing Gen X.
- If not present leaders now, they will be in the near future
- Expected to comprise 75% of global workforce by 2025[8]

Generation Z: 69 million

- Born 1997-2020—small percentage of the workforce at 5%
- A smaller generation of workers than its predecessors
- Many are just starting out in the workforce

As each generation's personal values and motivators change (in part influenced by the historical transfer of wealth[9] from Baby Boomers to their heirs), and as new technologies revolutionize industries, we'll continue to see an immense gap between talent demand and supply. The fact that the generation of workers larger than any other before or (foreseeably) after—Millennials—is already well established in the workforce, yet there are already roughly 10 million present job openings, is particularly foreboding. Gen Z does not have the numbers to fill the jobs being vacated by Baby Boomers. We can't predict future American jobs reports, but the trends

---

7. *Ibid.*
8. *Ibid.*
9. McKenzie Sigalos, "$30 trillion is about to change hands in the US," *CNBC*, July 10, 2018, https://www.cnbc.com/2018/06/28/wealth-transfer-baby-boomers-estate-heir-inheritance.html.

and generational math all but assure a huge shortage of talent—an exceptional impact that not even mass layoffs, artificial intelligence, nor immigration will be able to address.

Talent Planning cannot solve the talent shortage in America, but it will solve the shortage for *you*. This process will help you not only keep your current talent—and keep them happy and well-aligned in a fulfilling role—it will also make your business exceptionally attractive to job seekers. You'll become an employer of choice as word spreads about the life and career development opportunities your company offers.

Regardless of whatever's going on in the world, and whichever forces are rocking your competition, we can't let the talent we *don't* have diminish the talent we *do* have, or we'll waste valuable potential, costly momentum, and irretrievable progress. When EnzoPac's top problem was the consistent inability to staff or keep the right talent in the right positions at the company—which forced us to admit to ourselves The Old Way wasn't cutting it. We embraced a new mindset, recognizing the need to treat our talent issues as we would any other issue affecting our bottom line and put a plan around it.

Talent Planning lets us take control where we thought we were powerless; to be proactive where we have only ever been reactive; and to be assertive where we used to be passive. No more waiting for the right people to come around, or hoping the right people get on and stay on the right path at your company. Don't leave your business' future to chance; get the right plan and get (and keep) the right people to execute it.

It's time to make plans for your talent, instead of letting talent problems wreck your plans.

The Future of Talent

A key consistency I've gleaned from 25-plus years as a strategy & talent planning advisor is that people issues are always the top culprit derailing companies' growth. In the past, my less experienced self would've insisted a company's strategy is of the utmost importance—I've written this book because I learned firsthand the damage of putting that cart before the horse.

In the hundreds of companies I've led through the Talent Planning process, virtually everyone was still mired in the same self-inflicted diminishment and stunted growth that I'd previously recognized in my own company. I want to put this all-too-common problem in the past, and usher in the future of talent—Talent Planning.

The essence of Talent Planning is to grow your company by growing your people.

Now, it's easy to talk about putting the right people in the right place and giving our talent the tools to succeed and grow. But without an overall plan addressing every component of our teams, these noble pursuits fall flat:

- Costing us dearly as we leave valuable positions sitting unfilled—with responsibilities "temporarily" shifted onto others who may burn out from the added burden
- Squander hours and dollars on training bad hires
- Forced to employ costly recruiters to fill leadership positions because we failed to develop an internal candidate

This book will help you master the skill of Talent Planning—The New Way—to battle the people issues long plaguing your businesses. Talent Planning is not merely talent management, talent retention, talent development, or succession planning—the process covers all of these, though, and more as part of a grander vision for your business' success.

You can personally implement this process at your company with the guidance and tools of this book, or you may choose to bring in an experienced Talent Planning advisor to work alongside you, your leadership team, and/or your entire staff.

With Talent Planning you'll never again find yourself teetering on the backs of your heels, getting pushed backward by people issues, or blind-sided by predictable talent problems and generational shortages. Instead, this proactive approach to talent will hoist your company to a new level of growth acceleration as an employer of choice.

Are you ready to finally give your talent the serious plan they deserve? That your business deserves?

The next chapter discusses the basics of making a talent plan for your organization. Read on for a glimpse into the grand future of your company—one without people issues.

2

Our Talent Deserves a Plan

". . . I'm giving my two-week notice."

As a business leader, these are some of the worst words I've had to hear—especially when they come as a total surprise. How could I not have known a team member was *that* dissatisfied?

When business leaders are reactive to people issues, they can only sit back and wait to experience the cost and the drag of an unfulfilled or underperforming team member in their organization. You can expect to have these issues when you don't put proactive individual talent plans into place to prevent team members' dissatisfaction or departure.

I was always a strategy guy. When I was running a 5 million-dollar manufacturing company, my leadership team was glowing with excitement over the differentiated strategy we were rolling out, and expected massive profits to start rolling in. And yet, our initial growth stagnated not taking off like we planned. Why?

We didn't have the right people in the right places in our organization, and it was costing us dearly.

We needed an absolute change of mindset. If we have an issue costing us six figures off our bottom line, why haven't we put a plan around it? Why aren't we being proactive? Why aren't we investing in something so important to our success?

How humbling it was for me to recognize this blind spot. Why wasn't I treating people issues with the same seriousness I'd apply to any other issue slowing our company's growth? In spite of all the time and money I proactively invested into planning virtually all other aspects of the company, it never dawned on me to make a plan for our talent.

Thinking back on it now, it's hard to imagine being stuck in that old, reactive mindset. I shudder to think back to the days when our leadership team would simply ignore people issues, while carrying on without a clear, decisive talent plan in place. Beyond humbling, what an expensive oversight!

People issues may look slightly different from company to company, but they are painfully costly across all organizations. Whether it's a matter of talent deficiency or disengagement, people issues are the number one factor limiting companies' growth.

Talent Planning is how we can keep our talent engaged with and excited about their work. According to Gallup's State of the Workplace Report, employee engagement ranks at only 34% in the U.S. and Canada, while the financial costs of disengagement are ravaging companies. Per the Gallup report:

Lost productivity of unengaged and actively disengaged employees is equal to 18% of their annual salary

Replacing workers requires one-half to two times the employee's annual salary. So, if the team member makes 50,000 per year, it would cost 9,000 a year to keep each disengaged worker and between 25,000 and 100,000 to replace them.

Those numbers, however, only tell part of the story. Disengagement can be a symptom of talent misplaced within an organization—when people are working in positions that aren't a strong fit for their natural behavioral style and personal motivators. Getting your people in the best position to succeed is a core outcome of the Talent Planning process, ensuring they'll be engaged in their role and growing personally, while also helping drive company growth.

Talent Planning represents an investment in your people that yields numerous returns, including retaining your rock star employees, improving hiring and development practices, and further attracting new talent—particularly from other businesses who neglect to make talent plans.

During times when it seems like every other business or firm in town has its equivalent of a "Help Wanted" sign posted, with many offering competitive hiring bonuses and other lucrative incentives, it's all the more important for us to proactively retain and accurately recruit talent.

This mindset shift—moving on from what's familiar, yet ineffective—is an ambitious endeavor and, as is the case with any such undertaking, to be successful you'll need to create and work toward a vision for your business and talent.

The Process

Calculating the costs of a reactive approach to talent will shock any company into a change. As soon as my company recognized the profit and progress we were throwing away due to people issues, I began formulating the steps that would become the proactive Talent Planning process I'm sharing in this book.

The following seven steps are being adopted by new companies every month and for the sake of your company's growth, I hope you'll see the potential and highly practical value of leading your team through the process. Following is a high-level overview of the seven steps of the Talent Planning Process.

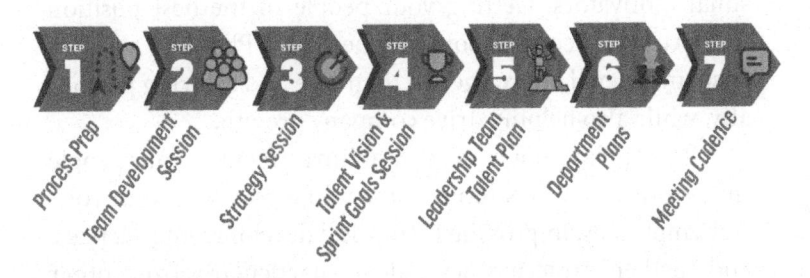

STEP 1: Process Prep
STEP 2: Team Development Session
STEP 3: Strategy Session
STEP 4: Talent Vision & Sprint Goals Session
STEP 5: Leadership Team Talent Plan
STEP 6: Department Plans
STEP 7: Meeting Cadence

Step 1: Process prep

First, identify the leadership team members who will make up this planning team. Decide who will lead the process—oftentimes this is the company leader—but not always. Get this team informed and up to speed on the Talent Planning process. Various roles and responsibilities are assigned here as well. Then, everyone will complete behavioral science assessments designed to increase self-awareness of natural behavioral styles, sources of personal motivation, and communication preferences. Everyone will prepare to present their life story, along with their behavioral style, using a questionnaire during the team development session.

Step 2: Team development session

Creating a brilliant strategy & talent plan requires a candid, transparent environment for discussion, where everyone is comfortable throwing our cards on the table. To understand the direction a team wants to take its company, they must first understand where they're coming from. In this step, individual team members get to know one another more deeply than ever through their story and behavioral style. The goal of this session is to get everyone comfortably brainstorming in a mutually open environment, enabling the team to have the difficult conversations that are necessary to solve the toughest issues and develop the best plan. With apologies to my friends in human resources, many have fondly referred to this exercise as "getting the team in their underwear."

Step 3: Strategy session

Here the team will create the bullseye for what the organization should look like in three years. This strategy will account for components uniquely subjective (such as differentiation, target market, product, services) and objective (such as quantifiable financial goals) documents, which are your strategic vision and financial vision. These two documents—collectively referred to as your strategy—will guide all decisions, including the talent plan.

Step 4: Talent vision & sprint goals session

This step leads to the functional organizational structure that needs to be in place to achieve the three-year strategic vision and financial vision. For example, if you are a 10-million company today and want to be a 20-million company by the end of your vision, what will your functional structure need to look like to support a 20 million company? After completing this future functional structure, the leadership team will define company goals for the first three- or four-month sprint. Then, action plans are defined to work on the business to achieve each goal.

Step 5: Leadership team talent plan

With the future functional structure established, the company leader develops a three-year talent plan for the leadership team, based on the information accrued thus far, as well as individual meetings with direct reports. This talent plan is the bridge leading the team from where it is today, to where it will need to be in the future functional structure to hit that three-year bullseye and achieve the strategic vision and financial vision.

Step 6: Department plans

Now the leadership team will present the strategy & talent plan to all team members, which in turn kicks off department planning. Department plans include: the financial vision, current organizational structure, talent plan, and action plans, with owners and due dates to achieve company sprint goals.

Step 7: Meeting cadence

With the Talent Planning process completed, it's time to develop an execution cadence of meetings to ensure continued growth for your company, but more importantly, for your people. The execution cadence leads to a culture of high communication and accountability.

Ownership of talent planning

Talent Planning is required for companies of any size, with any number of employees. Still, the scale of your operation does factor into who should take ownership and hold primary accountability for human resources and talent in your organization. Based on my experience working with businesses of various sizes, this is how I have seen companies typically handle these accountabilities (recognize that the categories below may fluctuate slightly based on what type of business you are and what industry you are in:

- **0-50 employees:** Since companies of this size typically don't employ a full-time human resources specialist, HR duties are of a more tactical approach. They may be outsourced with an administrative team member handling compliance, employee information, benefits, guidelines or handbooks, and attendance—the bare bones to operate legally. Strategic HR, on the other hand, includes responsibilities such as leadership and team development, hiring accuracy, and longer-term talent planning. At organizations of this size, strategic HR responsibilities and talent planning are owned by the company leader.

- **50-150 employees:** In this size range it's more likely for companies to employ a full-time, tactical HR specialist. However, the company leader still owns the strategic HR and talent planning responsibilities.

- **150+ employees:** Companies of this size can typically justify a full-time strategic HR specialist. When this is the case, and both tactical and strategic HR duties have been delegated, the company leader can focus fully on talent planning responsibilities. Though, ultimately, regardless of his or her company's size, a

> Ultimately, regardless of his or her company's size, a company leader owns Talent Planning because they own the strategy.

company leader owns Talent Planning because they own the strategy.

While talent planning requires a change in mindset throughout your organization, companies are increasingly recognizing the value in making this vital investment in their people now, up front, and proactively managing foreseeable people issues upstream. More and more of us are sick of sitting back and waiting for the problems to trickle in, knowing we'll painfully pay extra for our reactive passivity later on.

Chances are, if you're leading a company, you're not the type of person to just let predictable issues hit you, wave after wave, and do nothing about it.

No, I'm guessing that's not you. You're likely more of a visionary. In which case, pause for just a moment and envision your company free from people issues. Picture that, and think on it for 10 seconds.

...Pretty incredible, isn't it? Just *think* of the unprecedented growth your company could achieve in that productive state, unhindered. If your organization is a nonprofit, imagine the level to which you could advance your mission.

If you're ready for this mindset shift, finally fed up with the same old people issues, or even if you're currently experiencing new, unprecedented staffing problems, it's time to be part of the future of talent: Talent Planning.

Process Prep

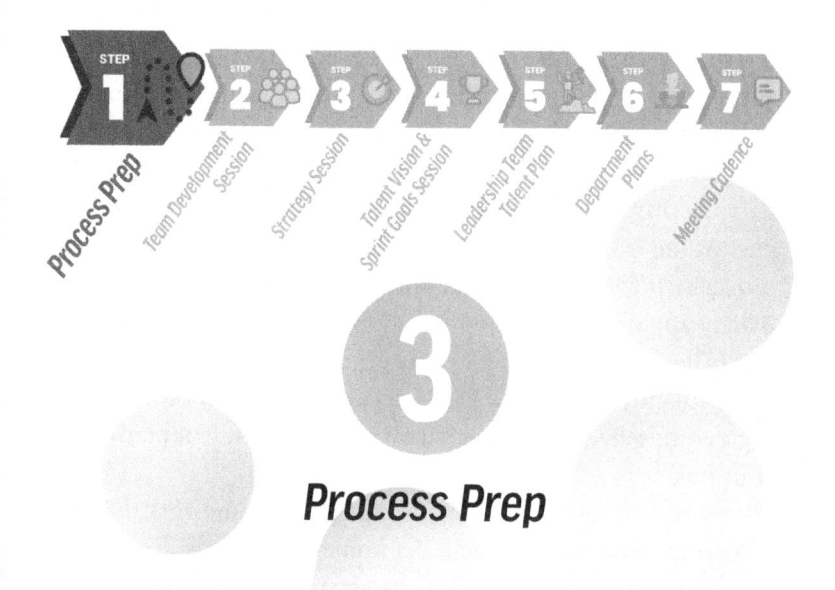

I recognize that you might be hesitant coming into the process—it's only natural. But based on my experience, I encourage you to trust the process. It's been repeated and refined hundreds of times to make it simple by including the essential components and eliminating any extra steps. It requires an initial effort from the leadership team but once you get into your meeting cadence in Step 7, you will start accelerating growth.

Your Pre-Launch Responsibilities

First, as a leader, you've got to personally understand the basics of the Talent Planning process. I would recommend reading this book in its entirety, then referring back to it as you advance through the seven steps.

Second, decide who will take ownership of leading your company through this process: the company leader? An internal team member? Or perhaps a trained talent planning advisor? Depending on the organization, not all business leaders are ideal to head up this process, but ultimately, only the business leader can make that determination.

Third, you'll need to identify exactly who will be a part of the leadership team, with whom you'll complete this process. In some companies, these selections will be immediately apparent, but others may have some tough decisions. Regardless, take the time to ensure you are assembling a team that can and will provide all the feedback necessary for creating a comprehensive strategy (and, ultimately, talent plan) for your business.

Last, break the leadership team into homework teams of two to three people each. As homework teams complete their prep for Step 3, which is the strategy session, and then Step 4, for the talent vision and sprint goals session, it provides team members with the strategic thinking time in advance to bring their best and most creative ideas to the sessions. Homework teams make the Talent Planning process very efficient while developing the optimum strategy & talent plan for the organization. Add some fun to the process by having each group pick a team name and engage in a little friendly banter on which team is going to bring the best strategy & talent planning recommendations to each session.

With these initial responsibilities taken care of, the next step is to schedule a one-hour (approximately) process launch meeting with this leadership team. In short order, you'll be experiencing some of the most exciting moments you've ever had as a company—the kinds of breakthroughs that leaders yearn for.

PROCESS PREP

The Process Launch

If you'll be leading the Talent Planning process at your company, don't worry if you're more pumped up for this first meeting than the rest of your team, so be it; after all, you have a much better idea of what's in store. But when you first gather the leadership team together and explain the overall concept, with every bit you reveal, they'll understand your excitement.

The basic essence of what you'll convey: "We are going to get more done with the right people and strategy by implementing Talent Planning. Since we put plans in place for all other issues facing this company—not to mention issues in our personal lives—it's time we finally put a plan around our people. This process will make us a much stronger team and help us formulate a talent plan to accelerate our growth like never before. The time we spend on Talent Planning now is just a fraction of the time future people issues would cost us."

You'll then provide an overview of the Talent Planning process.

Once your team has grasped the overall steps of the process, take the opportunity to schedule out the forthcoming sessions and dates for each step. The recommended duration between sessions is two weeks, which can admittedly be a bit aggressive, but waiting any longer than four weeks can put you at risk for momentum loss. Note that Step 6—department plans—is slightly more involved, meaning you will want to allow three to four weeks to complete it.

One final task (before you get to the fun stuff) is to assign specific team members the duty of preparing the analyses necessary for Step 2—a financial review and a market research summary. We'll address the exact purpose of these analyses in the next chapter, but the process launch meeting is the time to make sure your assigned team members will have these two reports ready for the next step in Talent Planning to present during the team development session.

The financial review is essentially a report of the company's current financial situation, and anything else pertinent to the financial outlook. For example, i.e., "target market A has a 10% higher gross margin than target market B." Such information will guide the strategy you'll be working to formulate, i.e. "We should get more of target market A's customers."

The market research summary entails an external survey of competitors and marketplace trends. This analysis will inform you on emerging trends in and related to your industry which might impact the strategy & talent plan you'll be developing.

With this business in order, it's time to move on to one of the most satisfying and fascinating portions of the process.

Behavioral Assessments

How can we really talk about the talent in our organizations? How can we talk about our people—and how can we be talked about by other people—in a productive and insightful manner, that's genuinely helpful *and* respectful? How can we talk about a person, *to* that person, without him or her taking it personally and getting defensive?

Behavioral science allows us to hold up an objective lens, through which we can examine our natural behavioral styles. Every one of us has a natural style that's largely developed in our teenage years, typically changing little throughout the rest of our lives. Quality behavioral science assessments provide us with this accurate, illuminating self-knowledge. With our styles being pretty well set since our teens, and the way the information is presented to us with a reliable, matter-of-fact report, it is shockingly easy to discuss our natural behavioral styles in front of others. Not to mention, it's thrilling to read such a report on one's self.

For example, DISC is an acronym for the natural behavior traits it measures: dominance, influence, steadiness, and compliance—reveals to us how we work, collaborate, and communicate. The assessment can be completed in less than 20 minutes, and you can just imagine how much it can teach us about ourselves.

DISC Graph

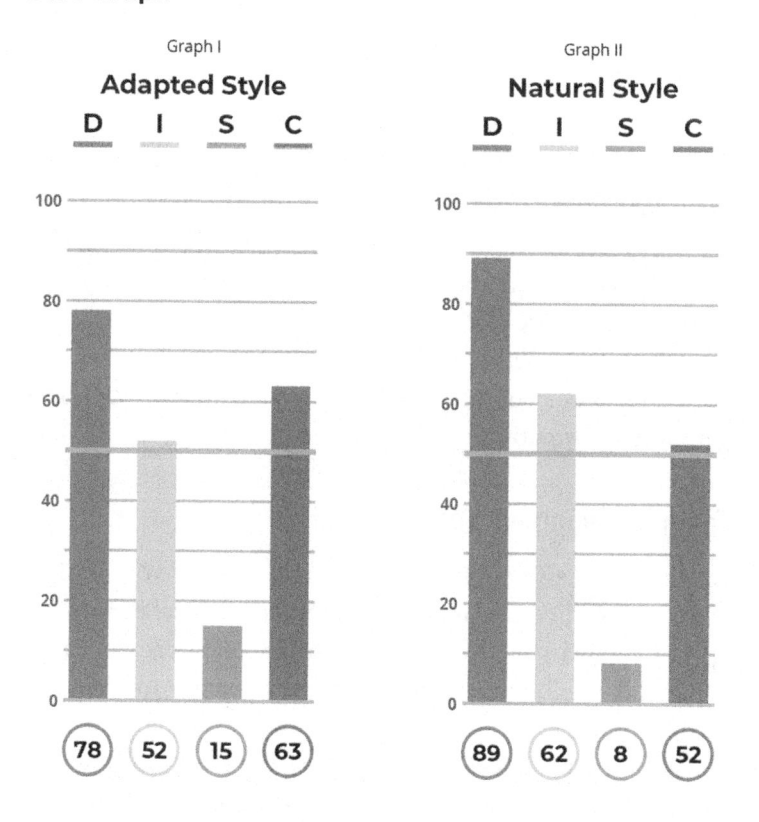

Graph I

Adapted Style

D   I   S   C

78   52   15   63

Graph II

Natural Style

D   I   S   C

89   62   8   52

As you can see in the example above, behavioral science gives us a common language, and effectively quantifies our natural traits, paving the way for transparent and vulnerable discussion on a delicate subject like interpersonal behavior. Assessment results make it much easier to have the tough conversations you'll *need* to have among your team. Behavioral science moves the conversation from defensiveness to development. The stronger the communication across your team, the stronger the strategy you'll develop together for your business.

When everyone completes a behavioral science assessment, all are put on the same level, with insights into our natural styles being revealed equally across the team.

You can implement the Talent Planning process whether you decide to use behavioral science assessments or not. But, frankly, I strongly recommend utilizing assessments because they enable the team to have the vulnerable discussions they've never been able to have before. Simply put, there's no better way to enhance team development and make every conversation more real.

We have a plethora of behavioral sciences. Reach out to your advisor, or contact us at info@mytalentplanner.com to get more information.

Team Development Questionnaire

In Step 2 of the Talent Planning process, you and your leadership team will be discussing one another's natural behavioral styles (whether you're opting to use behavioral science or not). Distribute the following questionnaire to each team member in the process launch meeting, with instructions to complete it within a few days—certainly before the next meeting, but the more time to reflect, the better. These questions help each team member present his or her style in the team development session in Step 2:

1. What are the strengths of your behavioral style and experience that that we need to leverage?
2. What are the growth opportunities or blind spots of your behavioral style that could impact the performance of the team?
3. How do you feel others in the organization perceive your style?
4. To communicate most effectively with you, what are the top things you ask others:
   - To Do:
   - Not to Do:
5. What is your vision for the leadership team? What characteristics, rules of engagement, or processes of a high-performance team need to be implemented in your team moving forward to optimize its performance?
6. What specific leadership development action plans are you going to take in the next 12 months to increase your professional and personal performance, and build a stronger and higher performing team? (These will be considered for your leadership development plan.)

Each member of this Talent Planning team must complete this questionnaire ahead of the team development session and come ready to discuss their answers with the group.

Final Tasks

Additionally, each team member must prepare to share his or her life story to the rest of the group. Pictures or other scrapbook items are particularly effective for this task, so encourage your team to bring in anything that will add impact, depth, and personal touches to their stories.

Inform your team that everyone will have a turn at the front of the room to present his or her story *and* natural behavioral style (ideally with assessment results shown on screen), before engaging in a discussion about his or her answers to the team development questionnaire.

With each of you preparing to put yourselves out there in front of everyone else, you'll already notice an initial shift in the dynamic and mood of your team. This is an early return of the process, yet it's got nothing on the breakthroughs coming up next.

Checklist

Leader's tasks pre-launch

- ❏ Understand the Talent Planning process
- ❏ Decide who will lead the process
- ❏ Identify and invite team members to the process
- ❏ Define homework teams
- ❏ Schedule one-hour process launch meeting

Leader's tasks at launch meeting

- ❏ Provide overview of Talent Planning process
- ❏ Set all dates for the process

- ❏ Assign owners for financial review and market research summary
- ❏ Provide instructions to complete behavioral science assessments
- ❏ Distribute the team development questionnaire.

Team's prep for Step 2

- ❏ Complete behavioral science assessments
- ❏ Compile financial review and market research summary, as assigned
- ❏ Complete team development questionnaire
- ❏ Prepare visual aids for telling life story
- ❏ Get excited to share and discuss life story, natural behavioral style, and team development questionnaire with the group
- ❏ Be ready to become a high-performance team

Team Development Session

Team development marks the first of three sessions—Steps 2 through 4—that are essentially full-day meetings. And believe me, these three days will be among some of your favorite days you'll experience at your company; days you'll look back upon and recognize as a turning point for the success of your business.

Admittedly, these sessions weren't always so enjoyable, or productive. From my time at EnzoPac when we developed a home run strategy for our business, I had known firsthand the powerful potential of getting a company's brightest visionaries in one room of focused collaboration, combining their creativity. I'd witnessed and personally experienced the incredible thrill that surges through a team when they're not merely pooling ideas, but multiplying them, building off one another. I'd been a part of a tightly knit team that constructed something together unlike anything else that had been attempted at EnzoPac, and I'd seen a new level of excitement that could energize the whole company and send our sales through the roof.

But what I'd failed to appreciate was how this strategy could *only* have been borne of a leadership team that was a real team: comfortable, conversational, empathetic, understanding, and perhaps most importantly, focused on a singular vision for the company.

It was only after I became a strategy & talent advisor—with hopes of helping other companies achieve the types of breakthroughs we'd had at EnzoPac—that I recognized how I'd underappreciated how integral our leadership team's communication had been to our success.

That chemistry and rapport I'd enjoyed, or perhaps even took for granted at EnzoPac, struck a healthy balance between candor and caring for one another.

When I started advising professionally in 1999, it was clear when I'd get a leadership team together in one room that the team was just not ready or able to have tough conversations. These teams would come into the sessions knowing they'd need to dig deep and put themselves out there in order to get anything done. Still, team members were hesitant and holding back.

Was what we had at EnzoPac so special? It couldn't have been unique to us—all teams have the potential to achieve that vigorous energy we had worked up.

In fact, taking off my rose-tinted glasses, I could recall some unresolved tensions and disagreements on our team that certainly didn't help our operation. Suddenly, I couldn't help but look back and think of how much more we might have accomplished if we'd have been able to go through a proper Talent Planning process.

Rather than dwell, this motivated me to ensure my clients would develop individually *and* as a team, and excel to their fullest potential unencumbered by poor communication.

I recognized that some of this ineptitude stemmed from an underlying and unresolved conflict on the team. Or, that someone may have a previous issue that's weighing down their figurative backpack—something they can't help but hold on to, and perhaps for good reason. It could be that some team members simply don't understand each other. Or maybe there's a new member of the team that we didn't really integrate yet, perhaps because he or she had been onboarded remotely.

As I witnessed teams incapable of openly engaging in difficult but fully necessary conversations, I determined that if there wasn't already an atmosphere in place that encouraged honesty and vulnerability, that we'd need to intentionally cultivate those qualities early in the process. It was that, or we'd never even get the strategic process off the ground.

What follows is the surest procedure to loosen up, energize, and strengthen your team. To create the strategy that will accelerate unprecedented growth for your business, you've got to first make sure your team is coming in HOT—which stands for honest, open, and transparent.

HOT Stuff

As you well know, the performance of your team dictates the performance of your business. In this step of the Talent Planning process, the performance of your team, and their ability to create a winning strategy for your

> The performance of your team, and their ability to create a winning strategy for your business, is dependent upon the level of communication—HOTness, even—among your leadership team.

business, is dependent upon the level of communication—HOTness, even—among your leadership team.

Together you'll define what success looks like for your company and plan the path to get there, including a plan to ensure your organization's talent has what they need to succeed. This will help employees throughout your organization grow as people, which will, in turn, promote growth in your company.

This idea sounds simple enough, and the process has been suitably streamlined to efficiently bring it to life.

Your preparatory actions in Step 1 signaled the launch of Talent Planning. The work you've put into introducing your team to the concept of natural behavioral styles is incredibly beneficial in and of itself, providing your talent with the type of self-knowledge that will inform their successes personally and professionally. But the real prosperity for your business is yet to come, as you build off of this powerful foundation.

Here in Step 2, the goal of the team development session is to foster the type of conversational, cohesive, and caring environment that will lead your team to unprecedented communication and decision making, enabling you to create a killer strategy for your company in Step 3.

As I've said, the only way a company can create a killer strategy is to be willing to have tough conversations. For example, if your company's sales are not hitting their targets, this won't be easy for your team to talk about when your sales manager is right there in the room. Or, if two people from the leadership team have historically butted heads and sewed division amongst your team, clearly, you'll need to resolve that conflict in order to unite on a singular vision for your company, awkward as that conversation may be. Or, the big one: a chronic lack of accountability across the organization.

All that potential finger-pointing... of course no one *wants* to have that talk.

However, as difficult or dreadful as such conversations may seem, you've got to power through them for the sake of your company. You must get your talent on the same page—and coming in HOT.

When leadership teams show up with honesty, openness, and transparency, *that's* when we can get real and overcome whatever's standing between our company and a record year. Being honest means, we treat each other with dignity and respect our team members by telling the truth. Being open means we're not keeping our thoughts to ourselves, but sharing our constructive opinions, unafraid of hurting feelings, driven by awareness that our ideas and wisdom are the life force of strategy creation—what will fuel our company's success. Being transparent means we're clear about our motivations and behavior, free of any sinister politics or ulterior motives, offering full explanations of the ideas we're proposing, and willingly inviting any questions for clarification.

So how on earth will you get a team of adult professionals to come in HOT? Honesty, openness, and transparency are not typically behaviors we adopt for people we don't know very well, and just because two people work in the same building hardly means they *know* one another, let alone trust or care for each other.

Again, if we want our team to come in HOT in Step 3, here in Step 2 it will be necessary to...

Get the Team in Their Underwear

Figuratively speaking, of course!

You've likely heard the common advice given to people who are afraid to speak in front of a crowd: "Picture the audience in their underwear." The idea is that a speaker will feel less nervous if they imagine the audience in a similarly vulnerable state. In the team development session, the goal is not dissimilar, although since everyone takes a turn speaking and sharing his or her own personal story, every team member is equally encouraged to feel comfortable in a collectively vulnerable state.

Each person on your leadership team will reveal his or her natural behavioral style (showing it on a screen for all to view), tell his or her life story, and share his or her answers from the Team Development Questionnaire. We learn here how a person's background has played into his or her behavior; in effect, why someone is the way they are. And this is what we mean by getting the team in their underwear—ridding the room of all pretense, and viewing one another with a new empathy and understanding.

What you're trying to do here is to develop your team and attain a higher level of functionality. The following session will intensely improve trust, commitment, accountability, and attention throughout your team, while encouraging them to embrace conflict as a means of overcoming obstacles that limit individual, team, and company-wide performance.

The Session

Before this session begins, the necessary tasks from Step 1 must be completed:

- ❏ Behavioral science assessments.
- ❏ Team development questionnaires.
- ❏ Prepare to tell your life story with pictures and props.
- ❏ Financial review, and market research summary compiled.

TEAM DEVELOPMENT SESSION

As everyone gathers for the team development session, you'll need to designate a scribe to take notes for individual development plans (more on that shortly).

To kick off this session in a big way, the company leader gives their presentation first. To do so is to lead by example, and there's no better way to break the ice then by putting themselves "out there" right off the bat is a powerful signal to the rest of the leadership team that, yes, all of us are doing this—even the boss is in "underwear." This only serves to enhance one's leadership, respectably coming across as a person who people *want* to follow.

If using behavioral science assessments, having one's results on a screen at this time is a tremendous aid to the presentations.

After the company leader, each leadership team member then proceeds to tell their life story—the past, all the way up to the present. It's up to each individual to decide just how much to share, but it is best to tell as much as one is comfortable disclosing. (The leader going first helps set the tone for the degree of transparency.) This vulnerable, candid expression of personal details is what will foster incredible interpersonal communication among the team.

You would be right to imagine how this can be a raw, powerful, emotional exercise. Listening to one another's stories, everyone's roles and even the office setting itself are momentarily forgotten, as suddenly you're simply there in a room having a great conversation. You may spend more time with these team members than you do your own family, and yet for the first time, you're genuinely learning about each other's backgrounds, and making sense of how each person's background shaped their natural wiring and motivations.

This is a chance for everyone to let the others know who they really are. What was growing up like? What was school like? What were/are your hobbies? How'd you meet your significant other? Do you have any kids? Showing all kinds of pictures is terrifically endearing and impactful.

Eventually, we want all team members to talk about their work history and where they are today, as well as the current personal and professional challenges and issues in their lives. Every one of us has fought and continues to fight our own unique battles, and though it may feel odd or uncomfortable at first, this is a special opportunity for our struggles and triumphs to be understood, while understanding those of others. This is the time to talk about you at your best *and* worst, as this is the story that has shaped so much of your behavioral style.

When people claim they don't have any issues, that's typically their first one right there. Everybody's got his or her blind spots, as well as strengths that developed while growing up. For example, I'm aware my father had low emotional intelligence, and I know that I picked up a ton of that from him. Suddenly, and empathetically, these stories lead to epiphanies as to why people are the way they are. And when you see people connect these dots for themselves in real time, that's when you'll see a team come together like never before. It's downright moving at times.

After sharing his or her story, each team member will present his or her answers to the team development questionnaire. This self-examination displays one's increased self-awareness. Further, when people bring up an issue they want to improve about themselves, it gives the rest of the team permission to hold them accountable. And, it makes it acceptable for others to talk about the issue with them.

Following this presentation, each team member offers one suggestion to the presenter, such as how he or she might perform at a higher level, or even just a tip on how to enjoy life more. Everyone in the room provides one of these recommendations of either personal or professional nature, and the team member up front has to consider this good-natured feedback, even if the recipient happens to disagree. Since everyone will take a turn in the front of the room, there's a built-in level of respect regarding this feedback. The scribe you designated at the beginning of the session takes down these suggestions, to be integrated into each team members' individual development plan.

As you continue through each presentation, you'll already take notice of changes in your team's dynamics. I've walked into rooms that were cold as ice, when teams are really struggling, stuck on organizational issues because they couldn't have the type of conversations needed. But by the end of the team development session, after everyone has told their stories and gotten input from the team, you'll have people who have barely ever talked to one another, now crying and hugging together. (Yes, this absolutely happens with adult men and women, and happens a lot.) This one session can improve the culture within a team and an organization within a single day.

Investing the time into this exercise is one of the most important things you can do at your company. In fact, the team development session yields tremendous benefits even as a stand-alone exercise, taking people from standoffish, to standing side-by-side with respect and compassion. But taken as part of the Talent Planning process, this session can really move conversations from defensiveness to development, and from closed-off to candid. This new strength will pay dividends in Step 3, as your leadership team is comfortable being bolder and more creative when strategizing, with a new sense of connection as you all work to develop and achieve a common vision.

Session Wrap-Up

After the final presentation, to help reintroduce everyone to reality, the respective team members who were assigned to compile the financial review and the market research summary will distribute and discuss their reports. These internal and external analyses will serve as the common sources of information upon which the homework teams (assigned in the process launch) will use to create a Strategic Vision for the company, to be completed ahead of Step 3.

Each homework team will complete the strategic vision and financial vision templates and present them at the next session.

What happens on the day of your team development session will define the culture for what your company accomplishes going forward. Enjoy the session for the incredible experience in and of itself, and cherish it for the breakthroughs it will provide in the next step: defining your company's strategic vision.

Checklist

Team's tasks for team development session

- ❏ Document leadership development priorities for each team member for their individual development plans
- ❏ Present life stories, behavioral styles, and team development questionnaires

TEAM DEVELOPMENT SESSION

- ❏ Give advice and recommendations to each presenter, to be documented by the designated scribe
- ❏ Financial review and market research analyses are presented and distributed
- ❏ Homework teams have the action plan to develop their strategic vision and financial vision (using the financial review and market research analyses) to present at the next session

Strategy Session

You didn't take your team through the breakthrough team development session just to turn around and put together some toothless phrase about how your company "will be the leading provider in the industry" and call it a day. Your job here in Step 3 is to define what you're actually aiming to accomplish: your vision.

Your typical vision statement is too vague to even know whether it's ever been achieved, completely lacking in benchmarks or measurability. In my 20-plus years as a strategy & talent advisor, I've learned time and time again that vision statements bring little to no value to an organization.

What does bring value is a clear and bold bullseye, a genuine target for where your company is heading in the future — a *strategy*.

Step 3 of the Talent Planning process is creating your business' strategy, which is composed of your strategic vision and financial vision. This strategy will drive all your organizational and operational decisions, particularly with regard to talent. Lacking this strategy, your team members across the company — from the front office to the plant floor to those out in the field — will lack the ability to make decisions that serve the true goals of your business. As leaders, we have a responsibility to paint that bullseye, big and bright, so all employees' daily actions and decisions will address one question: Does this help achieve our strategic & financial vision?

Target Practice

When everyone at your organization understands the strategy, each one is capable of bringing the business one step closer to accomplishing it. In this session, you and your leadership team will collaborate to craft a winning, definitive strategy. To formalize your target, your team will need to take a few practice tries while engaging in some extensive discussion.

These conversations can get heated, which is great: you'll want your team to come in HOT! The debates and drafts necessary for devising a killer strategy will require a lively blend of the honesty, openness, and transparency, which your team is now capable of (thanks to the team development session), as well as all the passion, creativity, and encouragement needed to forge the strategy that will inspire all team members for years to come.

The strategy session is, like the team development session, another all-day session, providing ample time to entertain various versions, consider input and presentations from each homework team, and allow everyone to give their best shot before compiling an ideal strategy — "practicing" until you've made that perfect target.

Also, similar to Step 2's team development session, the strategy session in Step 3 can make for a highly effective stand-alone session. This can be the case for your whole company or even just one department. Taken as part of the greater Talent Planning process, though, will truly unleash the potential of your strategy.

Ready...

The most important thing you can do to prepare for this session is to make sure your homework team is coming in prepared to work through the tough conversations. As I mentioned in the last chapter, our strategy session at EnzoPac was, in hindsight, hindered by the fact that we hadn't yet gone through a team development session and come in HOT.

The other expectation here is for the previously designated homework teams to have fulfilled their assignments and created their recommended strategy for the company. The homework teams' efforts will primarily fuel the conversations at the strategy session, and ultimately figure into the final strategic vision the leadership team sets for the organization.

Coming into this session, the homework teams will have already done a great deal of brainstorming together, and now they'll bring those ideas to the larger table for consideration. This pre-session preparation makes for serious efficiency in Step 3; the work done by the homework teams ahead of the session means team members have already had time to sort out and work through their thoughts, rather than taking the time to do this during the session.

With the leadership team assembled for this session, I recommend the process leader set the table with some rules of engagement:

TALENT PLANNING

- ▶ Put yourself in your teammates' shoes; actively listen from start to finish, *then* probe for clarity. You do not have to agree with what a person says, so much as try to understand it.

- ▶ What is said in this planning session stays in this planning session, unless we agree otherwise. There has to be an understanding that you can talk about anything in this meeting.

- ▶ Challenging a teammate's idea is healthy; attacking the teammate is not. If a person challenges an idea, it should not be taken personally. Healthy conflict and debate are signs of a high-performing team.

- ▶ Continue to build team trust by professionally handling any disagreements 1:1 with the individual, but outside the group. If the rest of the organization notices a rift, it deteriorates what the team is trying to accomplish. Understand that it all starts at the leadership team level. The organization will emulate how the team communicates, works together, and performs.

- ▶ Nothing's off limits; all issues must be addressed. Speak your mind or forever hold your peace. This is the place to put it all on the table.

- ▶ Turn off your phones, laptops, and other devices. Be fully present in the moment.

- ▶ Have some fun. Build a team, not barriers.

It's also good to keep in mind that for many members of the team, this will be the first time they ever had the opportunity to present their personal ideas and opinions on the direction of the company.

With that in mind, it's time to dive into the strategy session.

Aim...

At the start of the session, each homework team presents their strategy for the organization. This is as powerful as it is fun: we get to think big and talk about what we want this company to look like three years out, where we want it to be.

After each homework team has presented their strategic and financial visions and put all their creative ideas onto the table, the process leader facilitates one single vision using the content presented by the homework teams — essentially copying and pasting from each team's presentation and paring it down to a single strategy.

When it comes to solidifying your business' strategy, as big as the concepts may be, always strive to keep it simple. What you'll take out of this session, even after hours of conversation, can ultimately be boiled down to just two pages: the strategic and financial visions paint a subjective and objective picture of where you want your organization to be in the near future—i.e., three years.

Your leadership team will have to decide how far into the future you are going to aim. Most companies we work with create a three-year vision — not too far out, but certainly longer than just a year. I definitely have had companies who've chosen a two-year vision, particularly if they're in a highly technological, exceptionally fast-paced field. Other companies with a much longer product lifecycle, such as consumer goods or packaging, have found that a five-year strategy is more appropriate.

Still, three years is the most common span for a vision, and it's typically what I recommend, barring a strong rationale to adjust it. The three-year duration is so common that for simplicity, from now on I'll refer to a three-year vision;

if your company is using a custom duration, please mentally substitute that time span.

So, just what does a strategy entail? What creates this bullseye? What is that big idea that you want your organization to accomplish?

I recommend starting by designating a target 10 years out. I call this target the North Star. Again, this concept goes beyond some inarticulate vision statement. For example, I have one client whose North Star is based on the number of employees he'll have in 10 years. Many others, as you can imagine, base their North Star around revenue.

When I was at EnzoPac, our target was to be at 30 million in sales within 10 years. That became our North Star: our energizing, measurable number that we all looked to, that would signify the achievement of our potential, and true accomplishment for our company.

From there we worked down to the three-year vision. This bullseye is vivid, descriptive, accurate, and succinct.

There are two components to this vision: subjective and objective. The subjective components — aspects which only your company can define for itself, from its own, internal point of view — will represent your strategic vision. The objective components — concerning hard facts and data — will inform your Financial Vision. As you'll see, both sets of components are critical to zeroing in on your organization's bull's eye.

Strategic Vision

When building your strategic vision, there are eight questions to answer:

STRATEGY SESSION

Question 1: What is the competence/differentiation of your company?

Why would a business or customer choose to do business with you instead of a competitor? What are you best at, or going to become the best at, by the end of your vision? How will you differentiate from your competition?

Differentiation is a critical part of a strategic vision. In my 25 years in working with companies, I've found that not enough leadership teams actually speak in these terms, or make defining their differentiation a priority. This is a missed opportunity; clear differentiation leads to significant growth and increased profitability. **When you produce something that other companies don't, or something that they can't provide at your level, customers are going to pay you more for it.**

The key advantage at EnzoPac that differentiated us was our ability to change over our production lines quicker than our competitors could. No other company was able to switch packaging lines faster than us; what we could do in one hour would take our competitors one or two days. So, we

EnzoPac Competence Hierarchy

Competence

> Service Driven
> Granular Dry Food
> Turnkey Manufacturer with
> measurably superior machine
> change over capabilities

Target Markets

> User Driven
> 100 Top Branded
> Food Companies

> User Driven
> Food Service
> Distributors

recognized and sought to bolster this unique strength, and invested more into our maintenance team to make sure we had the tools, equipment, and capabilities to have the fastest changeovers in the industry, and our target markets loved us for it.

As I've said, we grew our company from 5 million to 30 million in just five years — half the time of what we had drawn up for our North Star. The beauty of a solid strategic vision and its inherent focus on differentiation is that, even when you think you're dreaming big, or even too big for your company, sticking to the formula often leads to hitting your target even quicker than you'd planned.

Question 2: Who will be your prioritized target markets by the end of your vision?

I encourage companies to define your primary and secondary target markets.

Your primary target markets are the companies or customers that value your competency the most — the ones willing to give you more business and pay you the most for what you do, something that they can't get from anywhere else.

Your secondary target market, if deemed necessary, is another group who values what you do, but perhaps doesn't have quite as high a margin as your primary target.

Having too many target markets can dilute a business' efforts, so I recommend focusing at most on these top two, with approximately 70% of your efforts going to your primary target market, and 30% going to your secondary. At EnzoPac, for example, our primary target market was the top 100 branded food companies in the United States. That's it; that's who we went after. Identify who will be your company's defined, finite target(s).

Question 3: External (customer) perceptions

How do you want your customers to describe you by the end of the strategic vision? How do you want to be perceived externally?

At EnzoPac, we wanted customers saying things like, "They keep us in stock; they're reliable; they're easy to do business with; they never let us down; and when we need product, they get it to us." Then, on an annual or biannual basis, we would complete customer surveys to make sure we were delivering on how we wanted our customers to perceive us.

Question 4: Products/services

What products or services are you going to be offering by the end of your vision? This can be a very fun conversation for the team, brainstorming new products or existing product extensions within our competence to create new revenue

This is also an appropriate time to discuss products or services you may cease to provide or begin to phase out.

Question 5: Geographic markets we serve

Are you targeting your state and a neighboring state? Or the entire region that you're in? Or are you targeting nationally? Lay out which markets you're going to be serving in the next three years. Are you going to add a new region? Or go international? These are very healthy conversations for your team to hash out; you'll want to know what everyone across the leadership team will agree to.

Question 6: Company values/culture

Define the four to six values that shape the culture of your organization. How do you want your employees to describe how it feels to work there?

For example, when I work with behavioral science to identify team members' motivators, it is increasingly apparent that the younger generations in the workforce, in particular, are motivated by the concept of harmony, which absolutely extends to their expectations of workplace culture — balancing the professional and the personal.

Including the desired culture of your company into your Strategic Vision means that you'll put the goals and action plans in place to make sure your culture becomes a talent attraction and retention tool.

Question 7: Strategic initiatives

Which areas in your business are vital components to getting you where you want to be in three years' time?

For EnzoPac, that area was a laser focus on the top 100 branded food companies; if a customer came in from outside of that top 100, we really questioned whether we wanted to even take them on. We also highly prioritized our maintenance operation, ensuring we provided them all the equipment and training necessary for them to maintain, and even improve our changeover speed — we couldn't allow any competition to touch our differentiated competence.

Question 8: Additional descriptors

What else can help you customize your vision, and help you create a more vivid bullseye? If the questions above feel like they're leaving something out, put that missing element here. For some companies, this section could include an acquisition strategy.

This question is intended to catch any missing core descriptors, or any unaddressed unique aspects of your company or industry, to make sure that as much as possible you're making this vision your own, completely tailored to where your company is, and where you want it to be in three years.

Financial Vision

Now that you've completed the subjective component of your strategy, it's time to focus on the objective component — your financial vision. As you lay these things out for your company and get everyone moving daily in one, unified direction, it's incredibly powerful.

A financial vision consists of the five to seven metrics you've decided to monitor on a monthly basis. These are the metrics that indicate your strategy is working, and that the health of the business is improving.

Define the unique metrics most significant for your business. At EnzoPac, one of our major metrics was the percent of our sales that went to our target market, the top 100 branded food companies.

Once you've defined five to seven metrics, put a specific goal out for each of them for three years out. EnzoPac wanted 75% of our sales to be coming from those top 100 companies. That drove us every day, and we focused our limited resources on these companies that valued us the most.

The Strategy

When you bring your subjective and objective components together, you'll create the bullseye that you can consistently measure your progress against. In the Talent Planning process, you will compare your current standing to that bullseye at least once a month, and make sure you're moving in the right direction. If things are heading the right way, you know you can accelerate and push the gas pedal down a bit more. If not, you'll tweak your strategic vision to make sure to get things moving in the right direction.

Fire!

We all have bad days at our organizations, or a bad couple of days — say, missing out on a new customer, losing a customer, or some misfortunate beyond our control that threatens to knock us off course.

But what's great about having a strategy is that regardless of how bad a given day or even week can be, your organization knows the track it needs to get back onto to achieve its vision. Your strategy is like a magnet that always pulls you toward it, regardless of what is happening in the short-term. And when you're moving with clarity and the unified energy of everyone in your organization, all focusing on that singular target, you're going to get there.

> Your strategy is like a magnet that always pulls you toward it, regardless of what is happening in the short-term.

Going through this process with EnzoPac, we had to reset our strategy because we were so far ahead of ourselves; we arrived at our 10-year North Star in just *five years*. It taught me just how much our talent plan needs to be tied to our strategy, and it's why I share this process with all business leaders who possess the foresight, comprehension, and willingness to see how far they can take their companies.

At the end of the day, Talent Planning is as simple as you, your team, and your employees asking one, clarifying question: "Does this decision move us toward our vision?"

The Next Step

Step Four of the Talent Planning process is the talent vision & sprint goals session. For this session, the homework teams will again collaborate, this time to define the future functional structure they believe needs to be in place in three years to achieve your strategy.

Say you're a 10-million company today, and you want to be a 20-million company in three years. What would the functional structure of your organization need to look like to achieve this vision?

When creating this functional structure, don't think about the current structure, or which people are in which positions right now. Just think about what the structure will need to look like to execute that strategy. For EnzoPac, with the emphasis we were placing on our maintenance team as a key to achieving our strategic vision, we decided to add our maintenance manager to our leadership team; he was just too important to our strategy not to have him more involved. It was a unique situation, but a similarly unique move may be what it takes for you to achieve your vision.

Such are the types of ideas the homework teams will bring to the next session, with each planning to present to the group like they did in Step Three.

In addition to bringing their future functional structure, each homework team will propose three to five goals for the first sprint of your strategy. And I'll tell you right now: teams *love* talking about structure. The next session will be among the most lively and interactive of the process.

Checklist

- ❏ Complete strategic vision
- ❏ Complete financial vision
- ❏ Assign future functional structure and sprint goals action plans to homework teams

Talent Vision & Sprint Goals Session

Step 4 of the Talent Planning process just might be the liveliest session of them all. The talent vision & sprint goals session is particularly exciting because of the foundation you'll be building upon. By now you've come together as a true team and have used that improved communication to devise the optimum strategy. Here, though, we tie in the talent in your organization. This is where you'll begin to truly solve your people issues and unlock your business' potential to accelerate unprecedented growth.

You now have a vision in place for your company. It's time to put a vision in place for your company's talent, starting with its future functional structure.

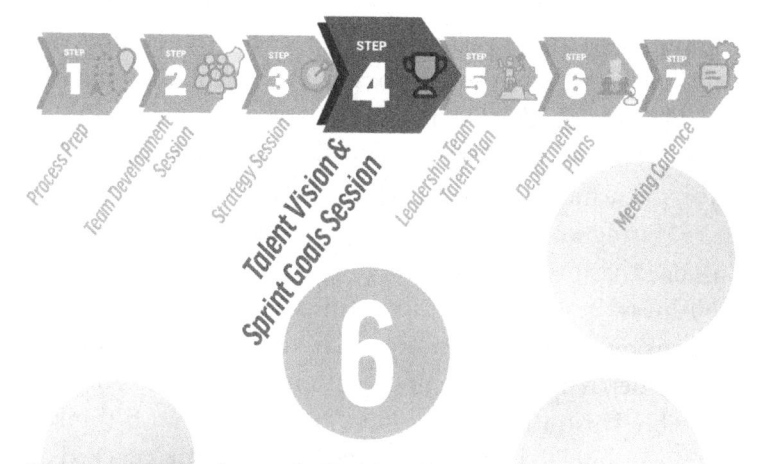

The future functional structure becomes your talent vision as you add more information to it, tuning it in with key accountabilities, and desired natural behaviors and motivators and more. Think of this future functional structure as the frame of a building you've dreamed up (a solid foundation), and the talent vision as the interior decoration (a more customizable project, based on that solid foundation). But with both, there is a common, essential question to ask yourselves: What does your talent need to look like in three years to achieve your three-year vision?

Firing up your new strategy is incredible, as you experience the thrill of this new, powerful momentum for your business. But without a future functional structure—and by extension, a talent vision—in place, your strategy is bound to be hindered by people issues. As I found out with EnzoPac, it's terribly frustrating to develop a brilliant, forward-thinking strategy, only to then have progress consistently knocked off-track by people issues. Creating a strategy is the most proactive undertaking that you as leaders can do for your company, but without tying in a talent vision, you'll be reduced to a reactive operation no matter *how* good your strategy is.

With Step 5 of the Talent Planning process, you and your team will take important steps toward creating the talent vision that will keep your company always moving forward, leaning into predictable people issues, and taking them on upstream, rather than waiting for them to sink your strategy. Your talent vision, combined with your talent plan, puts a full plan around any of your current or potential people issues, and keeps your company's growth accelerating the way you've envisioned.

The Session

Once again, the process leader will cede the floor to a series of presentations by the homework teams, only this time they'll be sharing the future functional structures they've prepared for this session. Remember, you want this to be an energized

TALENT VISION & SPRINT GOALS SESSION

and highly interactive discussion, loaded with constructive, good-natured competitiveness. Make it fun!

Structure is about two things—accountability and communication. Note how the future functional structure strictly focuses on positions and functions rather than containing actual names of current team members.

Far more important than knowing which specific people will fill the roles within this future functional structure, is the clarity of the roles themselves. Role clarity is one of the great inefficiencies to plague organizations, and with this session you will ensure role clarity in your Future Functional Structure: what exactly each role entails; the decision-making authority of a given role—its position in the "chain of command"—the three to five key accountabilities for a role, ranked in order of importance; and an estimate of how much time in a week to spend on each responsibility. Can you imagine how much this would improve communication at your company? It really brings teams together—and accelerates growth—when everyone has strategic clarity on where the organization is headed, and understands their role in achieving that vision (role clarity).

Starting with the board and/or company leader position and working through each department, each homework team presents the future functional structure they have defined to be in place to achieve the company's three-year vision.

What's often the case in these sessions is that some of the best ideas come from unexpected sources. For an example of how important this collaboration can be, I'll again cite my experience at EnzoPac. Our competence was so connected to our maintenance operation that we altered our functional structure to bring our maintenance manager onto our leadership team to represent his department, and it was arguably

TALENT PLANNING

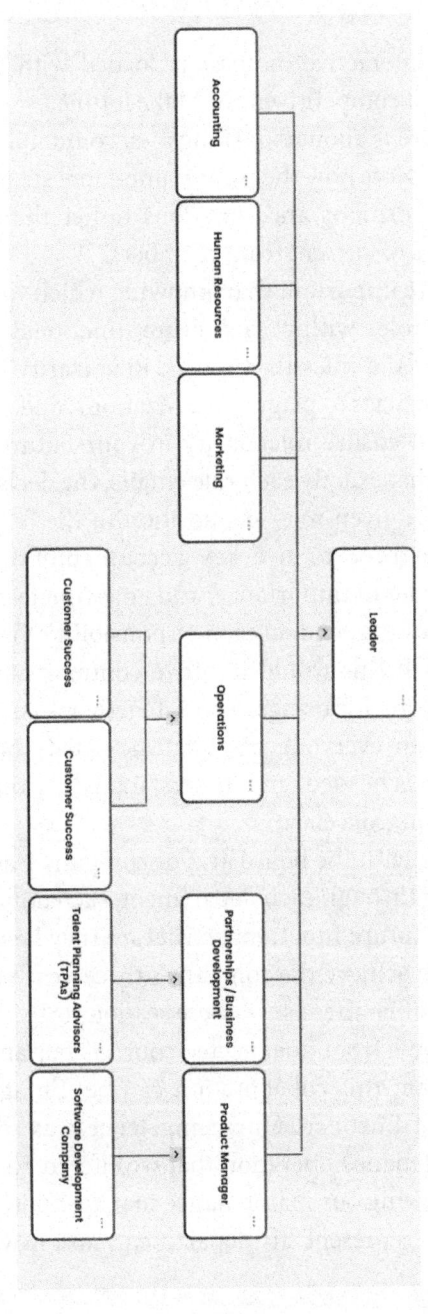

58

this stroke of genius that made all the difference to our success. This unusual yet brilliant idea didn't come from me; rather, it was an outside-the-box suggestion from one of our department leaders on the team. Frankly, without that specific idea, we may have never differentiated our business the way we did.

After each homework team presents their future functional structure, the full leadership team will discuss what stood out—even if all that stood out was how common certain ideas were across different presentations. But the unexpected differences between presentations can stand out just as much, and the group will talk through these differences as well.

As was the case in the last session on strategy, the goal here is to get all ideas onto the table for (HOT) discussion. This is all about coming to an agreement on the best possible, three-year future functional structure for your organization to hit its bullseye.

Prime Parking

All of this engaging discussion, which can make an exhilarating couple of hours, culminates with the creation of this future functional structure, but the brainstorming doesn't end there. There are always a number of outstanding action plans that come to mind after completing each significant decision or step of the Talent Planning process. Be sure to have a scribe note these ideas and stash them in a parking lot to revisit later. These items and areas, identified as a result of your future functional structure conversation, are places where you have identified a need for improvement such as new systems or processes, i.e. "If we're going to do X, it means so-and-so's going to have to do Y." As you go through this process, make sure you're capturing all of these valid items in your parking lot.

Too often, fresh ideas are easily forgotten after a conversation's passed.

When making these notes, I also recommend dividing action plans into two categories: *ActON* and *ActIN*.

ActON plans are those geared toward working *on* your business, such as conceptualizing a new process for the company or putting a new strategy into place—broader in scope, time, and implementation than your more regular tasks or routine to-do lists. ActON plans deal with advancing the organization, rather than getting a day's work done. In the next section you'll learn how to connect these to sprint goals.

ActIN plans relate to our day-to-day to work in our business. These are normal responsibilities we complete using the processes we've created and tailored to our operations.. ActIN plans are using those processes to complete your day to day tasks, such as shipping a customer's order, or making a sales call.

Both ActON and ActIN plans are important, and both need to be tracked, but they're very different—when you work *on* your business, you will get better at working *in* your business.

Sprint Goals

So far this session has focused on your talent vision. Now it's time to define your sprint goals—the three to five goals for your company to complete in its first sprint.

A sprint is a period of three or four months, based on whatever timeline your organization prefers. I believe that holding three four-month sprints is more effective because it allows teams more time to focus on execution; with three-month sprints, it feels like we only just finished planning, and we're already preparing for the next sprint. However,

TALENT VISION & SPRINT GOALS SESSION

many companies like to tie their sprint timetable to quarters. Decide as a team which sprint duration you prefer for your organization.

First, each homework team presents their recommended sprint goals to the rest of the team. The leadership team then agrees on three to five goals to to pursue. Next, the team will come up with ActON plans to achieve each goal. And for the sake of accountabilty, the team assigns an owner and a due date for each ActON plan.

Start by deciding what your organization is going to aim to accomplish over your first sprint. For example, here were our sprint goals at EnzoPac over a four-month period:

1. Increase annual sales to 8 million by focusing on our primary target market.
    a. Annual sales goal: 8 million
    b. Actual as of 7/31/XX: 6 million
2. Increase our gross margin percentage by strengthening our competence/differentiation and lowering costs.
    a. Gross margin = 23%
    b. Actual = 21%
3. Select and install new financial software system by 1/1/XX.
    a. Software selection by 6/30/XX
    b. Software not selected as of 7/31/XX
4. Enhance our culture through an team member survey and response plan.
    a. Complete team member survey by 6/30/XX
    b. Completed

Meetings cadence

Your final order of business for this session is what will ultimately justify all your efforts thus far: defining your meetings cadence. (Chapter 9 of this book fully explains the meetings cadence.) Talent Planning is not a one-off process, and your meetings cadence is how you'll see it through, as you construct a timeline of regular and highly efficient meetings to review your plan and tweak it as necessary. You'll want to set these dates out for the first year of your three-year strategy, and it pays to do it at this session with everyone in the room and ready to rock.

First, I recommend laying out a schedule for the leadership team to meet weekly, oftentimes holding them on Mondays can help set the tone for the week.

Second, you'll want to schedule monthly or bi-monthly plan execution meetings, when you will ensure the ActON plans you've all agreed to are getting completed.

Third, schedule weekly department meetings, perhaps on Tuesdays, so that you're consistently communicating the messaging from your leadership team throughout the rest of your departments.

Fourth, schedule sprint meetings to coincide with each of your sprint goals (every three or four months) to evaluate progress, make strategic adjustments and reset your goals for the next sprint.

Fifth, schedule company-wide meetings to take place within two or three weeks after each sprint meeting.

Last but not least, I recommend setting up monthly 1:1 meetings between each leader and their direct reports.

TALENT VISION & SPRINT GOALS SESSION

Session Wrap-Up

Hang on—take just a second and recognize how much work your team has accomplished at this point. Seriously! Over these first four steps of Talent Planning, and, in particular, with these last three sessions, you've made incredible progress as a team—personally, interpersonally, and professionally—and have mapped out a brilliant future for your business.

You've got a bullseye telling you where you're going, and how you'll get there. You've got unprecedented clarity from defining your future functional structure as your greater talent vision comes into view. And you've delineated a list of tangible, achievable sprint goals to knock out as the first step toward your vision. You've got to take at least a moment here and congratulate your team and yourself on getting all this together. This is powerful stuff!

With everyone's efforts appreciated and all due credit acknowledged, the Talent Planning leader should close out Step 4 by providing a look ahead at the final three steps of the process.

Leadership of the final steps will fall primarily on company leader—who will put the talent plan into place for the leadership team first, before then working with each of the company's department leaders to develop and implement the Talent Plan for each department. This is when Talent Planning really starts to take place in earnest, and it's what keeps a company from having to sit back and wait for people issues to gum up the works of their operation. This is how you'll mitigate the typical personnel troubles that would otherwise limit your company's growth, and what is shaping up to be a highly promising future.

Are you ready to put this plan into action? It's time to grow your company faster than you'd ever thought possible.

TALENT PLANNING

Checklist

- ❏ Finalize future functional structure
- ❏ Finalize sprint goals
- ❏ Define meetings cadence
- ❏ Provide overview of remaining Talent Planning steps
- ❏ Company leader prepares for Step 5 meetings with leadership team

The Talent Plan for your Leadership Team

The previous steps of the Talent Planning process have been remarkably collaborative. Here in Step 5, though, it's time for the company leader, who is the chief talent planner, to take the reins of the process in Step 5.

You've got your strategy. You've got your future functional structure. Now it's time to progress toward your talent vision and complete your talent plan.

The talent plan is the bridge that will transport your organization from its current structure to the future functional structure within three years, accelerating your company's growth with every step across.

You'll begin building this bridge right here in Step 5, by developing the talent plan for your leadership team. (You'll continue construction in the next chapter with Step 6, when you'll guide your department leaders in developing a talent plan for their departments.)

The Template

An important characteristic of defining your future functional structure in Step 4 was to disregard your current structure and not think about specific names—the goal was to focus purely on an ideal structure, and the roles it should entail to deliver your three-year vision.

In creating a talent plan, however, the opposite is true. In Step 5, the focus is absolutely on the actual people in your organization, and where they will best fit in the future functional structure.

This is where you'll envision what your leadership team needs to look like in three years to achieve your vision. When developing the talent for the leadership team, documenting the following will bring tremendous clarity and a series of wins for your organization:

1. **Strengths of talent/team:** What are you great at? In which areas are you the most solid? Which assets does your team bring that enable you to deliver your competence and stay ahead of your competition?

2. **Talent/team weaknesses and blind spots:** Where do you need to improve? What are your blind spots? What current talent challenges are you facing that your talent plan must resolve?

3. **High potentials you need to retain:** Who are your most promising team members, and how are you going to keep them?

▶ Retention has become so important, as we discussed in Chapter 2, but even more so, in light of the plan you've put in place. You can only enjoy the full, accelerated growth from your strategy & talent plan if you can hang onto your up-and-comers.

4. **Skillset gaps you need to fill through development or hire:** Which skills are you presently missing that you'll need in the next three years to achieve your vision? Are these skills lying dormant or untapped in your current team, or will you need to bring in someone new?

5. **Development priorities for each direct report:** In what order of importance do you address and fill the gaps in your collective skillset? How will you minimize or eliminate the weaknesses on your team? How do you go about leveraging the strengths on your team? What are the two or three areas for each team member that you should focus on developing, that will build the leaders and team capable of achieving your strategy? Keep in mind, we would always prefer to promote current team members before hiring external candidates.

6. **Prioritized promotions and/or new hires with timetable:** What's the order of promotions and/or new hires you're going to make over the next three years? How do you plan out and prioritize which position is filled first, second, etc.?

7. **Succession plans:** Which retirements are you expecting in the next three years? What plan do you

have to put in place to develop the right people to step into these roles?

8. **Action plans/notes:** What are you going to get done over the next sprint to keep you on track to hit your bullseye? This specifically refers to action plans of a confidential nature; all others would be attached to sprint goals.

Talent Plan Resources

Your next step as leader is to begin to construct a first draft of your talent plan. You'll want to switch gears and work on the leadership team talent plan as soon as possible to keep momentum into department plans. There's great value in doing this before beginning your individual meetings with members of the leadership team; the information and points of comparison you'll gain from these 1:1s can then help complete, confirm, or even constructively contradict your draft.

The talent plan template is just one of several resources available to better inform your draft. The following resources will not only add depth to the first draft of your Talent Plan, but in curating them ahead of time, they will also maximize the efficiency of your upcoming 1:1 meetings:

▶ **Your future functional structure:** This provides what the structure needs to look like to achieve the strategy providing direction for your talent plan.

▶ **Behavioral science results/team development questionnaires:** Certain behavioral styles are better fits for certain positions, and behavioral science teaches us how to best leverage different team members' natural styles. With behavioral science it can feel as if you're able to read someone's potential right from his or her printed report. Having familiarized

THE TALENT PLAN FOR YOUR LEADERSHIP TEAM

yourself with this information will also make your 1:1s incredibly efficient, thanks to your awareness of each person's strengths and weaknesses (not to mention the improved communication we gain from behavioral science).

▶ **Team wheels:** The behavioral science team wheels are a powerful visual representation of the makeup of your team which helps in developing your talent plan. Are we missing any skill sets or perspectives on the team? How can we turn potential conflict of our natural styles and motivators into a team strength through awareness?

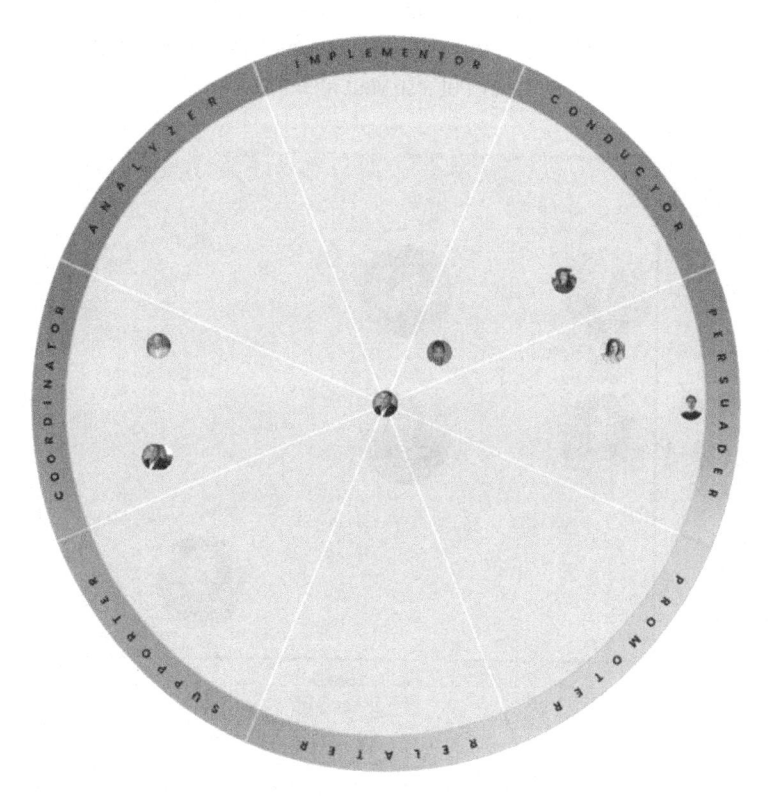

TALENT PLANNING

▶ **The 9-Box**: You may be familiar with this tool: a graph with potential on its y-axis, and performance on its x-axis. Completing a 9-Box and thinking in these terms ahead of your individual meetings will arm you with insight. For example, if you have someone who has high potential, but performs at a low level, you'll want to put a development plan in place for them. Or, if you have someone who has high performance, but medium or low potential, meaning they're doing quite well right now, what is your retention strategy to make sure you keep this person in-house and happy? These are all powerful considerations that would benefit not only the first draft of your talent plan, but also your meetings.

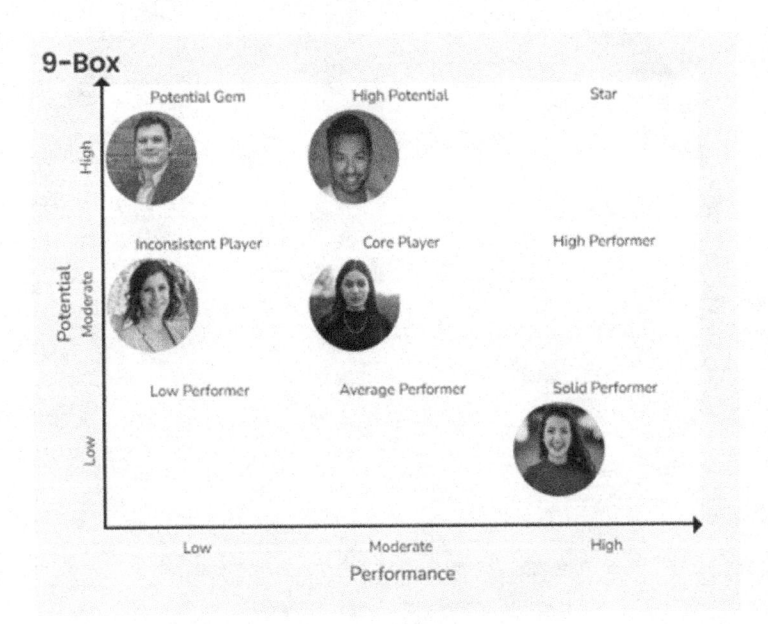

9-Box

	Low	Moderate	High
High	Potential Gem	High Potential	Star
Moderate	Inconsistent Player	Core Player	High Performer
Low	Low Performer	Average Performer	Solid Performer

Potential (y-axis) / Performance (x-axis)

The Meetings

Your next step as the company leader will be to meet with the members of your leadership team individually—ideally this is still within two weeks after completing the last session.

After all of the preceding group discussions and presentations, even in light of the team development session, you and the leadership team members may find it a bit refreshing to be back in a 1:1 scenario. Lean into that, and make these meetings honest, open, and transparent. The content of these private discussions, after all, goes no further than the two of you.

The emphasis here: Where can each team member bring the greatest value to the company and to themselves?

Read that last sentence again and take it to heart; this isn't just some fluffy, feel-good concept. The crux of talent planning is getting people aligned in their best role. When you work with someone to achieve this, not only does the individual feel positively energized, but that energy will then accumulate throughout your company and translate into accelerated growth. (See Chapter 10 for more on the concept of being a shepherd of the talent.)

Lay out a number of materials for the two of you to reference during these 1:1s, such as in individual's behavioral assessments/team development questionnaire, the company's strategy, and the future functional structure.

Throughout your conversations with leadership team members, you'll want to take notes with regard to completing your leadership team's talent plan, while looking to accomplish the following:

TALENT PLANNING

- ▶ A review of each person's natural behavioral style, its related strengths, and where those strengths bring the greatest value to them, and to the company.

- ▶ Understand the career goals and aspirations of each team member. "We've done all this talking about what's best for the organization, but what do *you* want to accomplish personally?" If you help a person achieve their life goals, they will help you achieve your goals for the company. Your talent plan must take into consideration how to help fulfill your leadership team members' aspirations, whether that can be achieved via your organization or not.

- ▶ Discuss (and certainly document) their top two or three leadership development priorities that will lead to excellence in their role. "How are you looking to improve? How can we invest in you and your success?" Though, again, this applies both professionally and personally—developing the total person.

- ▶ Discuss the future organizational structure in general terms. You want their input on what's working and what's not. This perspective and insight are hugely impactful when constructing a talent plan.

Your Talent Plan

After meeting with every member of the leadership team, you'll be flush with valuable new input to help finalize your talent plan.

In spite of all of the information, time, and effort that goes into a talent plan, this all still boils down to that one-page, eight-question talent plan template.

This finalization process is often handled solely by the business leader, particularly if they have determined one or more members of the leadership team are poor fits for the new strategy. The leader reserves the right to final say over the completed talent plan regardless, but in some cases he or she may find it beneficial to call the leadership team back for another group meeting to present the talent plan, and perhaps even solicit feedback in this group setting. Whether or not to seek this further input from the team is entirely at the discretion of the leader, and is entirely situation dependent. Ultimately, though, the leader will share this talent plan with the leadership team, along with a timetable for its implementation.

Finalizing a Talent Plan for your high-performance leadership team is an immense accomplishment.

Next, get ready for talent planning on a departmental level—when you'll get to share this wealth with the rest of your company!

Checklist

- ❏ Meet 1:1 with each leadership team member
- ❏ Finalize current structure with names
- ❏ Finalize leadership talent plan and implementation timetable
- ❏ Share talent plan with full leadership team

Department Plans

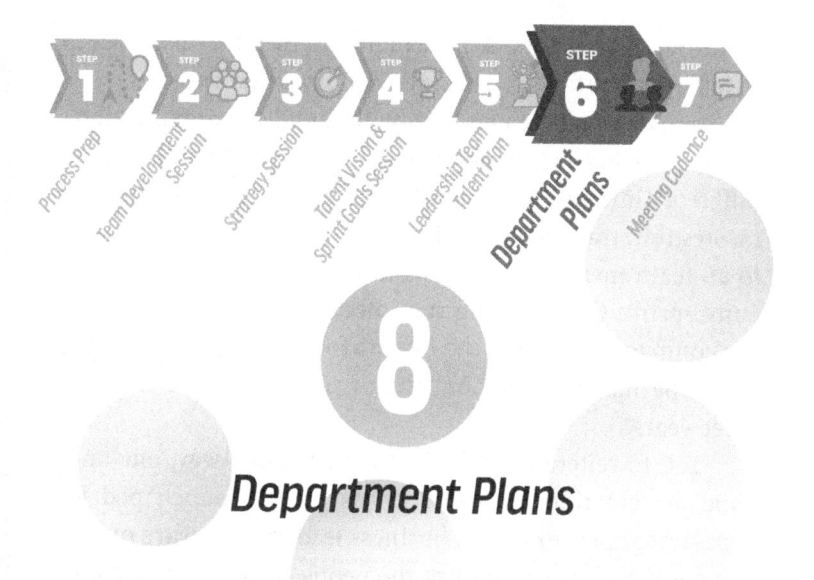

Now that you've solidified a multi-year talent plan for the leadership team, it's time to dig in where you can start turning your strategy into action: in your departments. But this step of the process is hardly just about delegating tasks. Step 6 is primarily about getting the entire company to work *on* the business, and not just in it.

Presenting your three-year strategy & talent plan to all employees is the first step of department planning. By sharing the newly developed vision and goals with the organization, you're on your way to creating the department plans that will hit your organization's bullseye.

The Presentation

Finally, the leadership team gets to share their progress on the strategy & talent plan with the entire organization, engaging team members throughout the company and drawing their input into the process. A presentation typically runs between 30-45 minutes, followed by a celebratory social event.

In a meeting area large enough for all the organization's team members (or, if necessary, over multiple meetings at different times and locations) the leadership team communicates the strategic vision, financial vision, and talent vision to all team members, along with the goals for the first company sprint. Chief among the information provided here is the company's bullseye, the filter through which all decisions are to be made throughout the organization over the next three years.

Yet, to reiterate, this is not simply a one-way, one-and-done presentation, rather much as it's the launch pad for department planning. We business leaders are aware of how many great ideas come from the people within departments who work most closely to the greatest challenges—the people who live and breathe these issues daily.

The purpose of the following agenda is for the leadership team to engage all team members as you embark upon building your department plans.

The Agenda

1. Opening remarks: Welcome all team members

2. Meeting agenda overview: Simply provide a summary of what will be covered in this meeting

3. The planning team: Introduce each member of the leadership team that has been working on the Talent Planning process, and has put the strategy & talent plan together as it currently stands.

4. The Talent Planning process: Explain the seven steps of the process with transparency to engage

everyone. Remember, it's inspiring for team members to know there's a vision for their company—that all their hard work is going toward something definitive—and how it was developed. Still, very few organizations have a real vision, and even if they do, they don't share it with all team members. This is your opportunity to fulfill two of the core responsibilities of leadership: strategic clarity, and role clarity across the organization. Communicating where the company is going and what everyone's role will be in this journey is how you'll get everyone working together and achieving the vision.

5. Review team development session: Yes, you should in fact tell everyone what you did for this exercise. You're building a culture of awareness and transparency. You will gain loyalty and respect with your team members by sharing with them an overview of this vulnerable process the leadership team willingly undertook.

6. Review strategy & talent plan: Present the following components:
   - Strategic vision
   - Financial vision
   - Future organizational structure
   - Current structure
   - Sprint goals
   - Meetings cadence

7. Review department plans process: Lay out the expectations and timetable; within three weeks, the department leader will come back and present their

department plan to the leadership team. In some cases, department leaders may bring other members of their team along to be part of this presentation.

8. Question and answer session/discussion: Expect that at this presentation your audience won't provide much feedback initially. I've done these enough times to know you shouldn't take it personally if your team members are confused and quiet at this first company-wide meeting; a concept like talent planning, and particularly how it pertains to them, doesn't always sink in right away. But the second time through this, you might get a couple of questions comments. And then the third and fourth times, it's more likely that you won't be able to get people to stop chiming in! You'll even start getting approached outside of meetings with suggestions from eager team members. Once they start understanding talent planning, people who may never have considered working *on* the business will start to share their innovative ideas. They'll understand the company's bullseye and the role they play in achieving this vision, and that clarity is absolutely energizing.

9. Hold company social. Again, you want to keep these meetings positive, celebratory even. Ending with a social event is the perfect way to kick off department plans.

What goes into a Department Plan?

The broadest goal of a department plan is to get more of your team working *on* your business—through ActON plans. In

DEPARTMENT PLANS

most organizations it's largely, if not exclusively, the leadership team who works on the business. But why limit the potential for ideas and contributions to just them? Department planning drives this level of execution throughout the rest of your organization, involving the people with intimate knowledge and expertise of daily operations from working *in* the business. (Improved ActIN plans will come later, naturally, and will be even more efficient in light of this expanded roster of talent working on the business.)

This holistic approach of department planning leads to organizations experiencing record growth. In total, a department plan includes:

1. **A financial vision:** Each department defines three or four metrics to measure the effectiveness of the department plan, typically monitored on a monthly basis. For example, in my time at EnzoPac, one of the metrics for our financial vision was our closing rate in the sales department. These metrics should also have objective, quantifiable goals attached; in our case, it was comparing our current closing rate to what we wanted it to be at the end of our three-year vision.

2. **ActON plans.** Define ActON plans for each goal, that each department is to complete during the next sprint that will help achieve the company's goals. Every action has a due date and an owner from the department to work *on* the business. This owner may certainly get help from others, but he or she is ultimately accountable for the action's completion. Most, if not all, of the members of a department should own ActON plans in every sprint. This is a key discipline for achieving higher and faster

company growth, and a huge win to take away from this step.

3. **Talent plan.** The company leader works with each department leader to create and update a talent plan for their department, using the same process and talent plan template used for the leadership team.

4. **Organizational structure.** Finalize the current department structure as you create and update your talent plan. On a departmental level, role responsibilities can get even less clear than on a leadership level, particularly with regard to hierarchy, i.e. "Who do I go to for help when such-and-such happens?" We want the structure and responsibilities to be clearly defined within our organizations, and the very act of clarifying a structure can often highlight any improvements or alterations that would benefit the department.

Developing a Department Plan

To further engage all team members throughout your organization with the strategy & talent plan, after the presentation the leader will begin to meet individually with each department leader to guide them through the creation of a department plan. Together they will work to shape and polish this department plan as much as possible, creating a strong first draft (as you did with the leadership team's talent plan), to be bolstered with feedback from the forthcoming meetings and discussions.

The department leader will set two one-hour meetings with their full department to complete the first two components of the department plan:

DEPARTMENT PLANS

- **Meeting 1:** Develop a financial vision with three-year financial goals for each metric.
- **Meeting 2:** Set ActON plans for each of these goals.

The department leader will then meet 1:1 with each of the members of their team to get feedback and work together on the third component of the department plan—the talent plan. Similar to the leadership team's Talent Planning process, these meetings also present an opportunity for the department leader to candidly engage direct reports regarding:

- Natural behavioral styles, and where the team member's style and strengths can bring the most significant value to themselves and the organization
- The team member's career goals and aspirations
- The team member's top two or three development goals, to be discussed and documented

Finally, each department leader then presents their department plan to the leadership team for finalization and feedback, and to ensure alignment across the organization. The leadership team helps shape each department plan to achieve sprint goals and take another step toward fulfilling the three-year vision.

With department plans now in place, your organization is ready to execute like never before, and reap the rewards of your strong planning efforts as your business' growth accelerates with unprecedented speed.

Believe it or not, there's just one more step to the Talent Planning process: establishing a meeting cadence to ensure your organization continues to execute your talent plan and achieves your three-year vision.

TALENT PLANNING

Checklist:
- ❏ Complete plan presentation
- ❏ Complete department plans
- ❏ Present department plans to leadership team
- ❏ Finalize annual budget
- ❏ Update goals for financial vision

Meeting Cadence

You've now completed some of the heaviest lifting you'll ever do on behalf of your organization. Creating a strategy & talent plan requires focus and energy, and I hope you took a moment to appreciate that. But now it's time to make it happen.

Step 7 of the Talent Planning process—setting your meeting cadence—is how you'll make your vision a reality. This ongoing effort is how you'll commit to hitting your bullseye, by setting regular goals, action plans, and metrics throughout your three-year vision.

Now, before your eyes glaze over at the mention of more meetings, let's take a step back and reclaim meetings as the positive collaborations they're supposed to be. When people think they hate meetings, what they actually dislike are ineffective meetings: undefined agendas, poor organization, aimless discussions—meetings for the sake of meetings, where not only is nothing new accomplished, but we've just lost time that could have been much more productive. We all know how that waste of time can breed stress and resentment.

In reality, we get a unique thrill from focused collaboration, especially when it leads to new ideas we could've never discovered on our own. Effective meetings are also a vital, regular opportunity to celebrate wins and appreciate each other's efforts.

Still, you may be thinking...

Do we Really Need these Meetings?

I don't blame your skepticism, but the answer is an emphatic yes. Moreover, you'll actually want to have them—seriously!

One of the greatest impacts from the culture change of the Talent Planning process is an all-new enjoyment of meetings in your organization. And really, it makes sense that businesses that haven't gone through Talent Planning would have dreadful meetings; after all, who wants to sit in a room full of unresolved people issues, inhibited with poor communication, and lacking a solid sense of the business' goals?

With Talent Planning, your strategy & talent plan has proactively paved the way for smooth communication, unity, and clarity en route to your three-year bullseye, making for outstanding conversations. The enthusiasm your team will experience leading up to these meetings may only rival the excitement they feel after these powerful collaborations.

You'll keep this positivity and productivity rolling by way of a meeting cadence—a consistent set of focused meetings to get into and maintain a rhythm throughout your organization, ensuring effective communication, accountability, the execution of your plan, and ultimately, the successful achievement of your vision.

Think about it. We regularly schedule all sorts of check-ups, tune-ups, and appointments—we schedule our personal fitness cadence to meet our fitness goals and keep us on track, and make sure we get our cars' oil changed, for example.

It only makes sense that we'd create a cadence to check up on the status of the most important factors of our businesses' success: our strategy & talent plan.

In Talent Planning, your meeting cadence is a regularly scheduled series of efficient meetings. (These meetings are scheduled at the end of the talent vision & sprint goals session in Step 4.) For each meeting, your cadence defines:

- ▶ **Who** will take ownership or responsibility of scheduling and agenda duties
- ▶ **Who** will attend
- ▶ **What** to discuss
- ▶ **When** and **where** the meeting will take place
- ▶ **How** long the meeting will last

With a reliable and clear meeting cadence, all team members have the assurance that they're going to get consistent updates, and have regular opportunities to ask questions, provide input, and altogether engage with the execution of the plan. I call this communication clarity.

Your Meeting Cadence

What's your ideal rhythm for effective communication, and to ensure the ActON plans and commitments are getting done? Not only will you need to keep the necessary pace to achieve your vision within three years, but everyone involved must be clear on and comfortable with this cadence.

Your meeting cadence may be uniquely tailored to your business; cadences are often dependent upon the size of a business. However, based upon best practices from working with thousands of organizations, the following six meetings (held at the frequency suggested) lead to exceptionally high performance for teams committed to the Talent Planning process.

Note: Suggested agendas and advanced tips for each of the following meetings are available in the Appendix at the end of this book.

1. Leadership team meeting

A weekly leadership team meeting builds team cohesion, resolves internal or customer issues, makes decisions, and sets priorities for the coming week, that each leader communicates to his or her teams across the organization. A business is only as effective as its leadership team, making these meetings essential to great execution.

- Who owns it: The company leader
- Who attends: The leadership team
- What to discuss:
    - Cultivate connection; make strategic decisions
    - Establish weekly priorities
    - Decide what needs to be communicated to the rest of the organization
    - Solve any issues; and ensure accountability
- When to have it: Weekly. At my current organization, and as we did at EnzoPac, we hold leadership meetings at 8:30 a.m. every Monday to set the priorities for the week.

- Where to have it: In a conference room, and/or via videoconference.
- How long it lasts: The recommended duration is 60-75 minutes.

2. Plan execution meeting

These are among the most important internal meetings for excelling at execution. We usually see this meeting happening monthly or every two weeks, with a primary focus of ensuring all team members are completing their committed action plans.

- Who owns it: The company leader
- Who attends: The leadership team
- What to discuss: These meetings foster and create a culture of consistent accountability that accelerates the growth of the organization and leads to outperforming competition. The objectives are to:
  - Review execution of the plan to date
  - Review financials, look at performance compared to budget
  - Ensure accountability of ActON plan due dates
  - Make any necessary strategy & talent plan adjustments.
- When to have it: Bi-weekly or monthly—whatever is more appropriate for your company. Many companies will hold this meeting directly following one of their leadership meetings.

- Where to have it: In a conference room, and/or via videoconference.
- How long it lasts: The recommended duration is 75 minutes.

3. Department meetings

Keeping each department connected and on the same page is vital to the health of your organizatioon's culture. Personal updates are as important to these weekly or bi-weekly meetings as are discussions of where we are at on our action plans.

- Who owns it: The department leader
- Who attends: The department team members
- What to discuss: This meeting is when the department team meets to connect, communicate, and ensure progress on the department plan. The objectives are:
  - Team building
  - Providing company updates and announcements
  - Developing department action plans and priorities.
- When to have it: Weekly or bi-weekly—I recommend companies hold their department meetings every Tuesday after the Monday leadership team meetings. What is decided in leadership team meetings can then be efficiently communicated to the departments.
- Where to have it: In a conference room, and/or via videoconference.

- How long it lasts: The recommended duration is 60-75 minutes.

4. Sprint meeting

In a fast-pace business, having an agile, adaptable planning process is essential for pivoting when necessary. Executing plans in three-to-four-month sprints allows for assessing and regularly updating your strategy & talent plan, as well as setting the goals for the next sprint. Each of these leadership team meetings is held offsite for a half-day session, marking the end of each sprint and beginning of the next, and representing another step toward achieving your vision.

- Who owns it: The company leader
- Who attends: The leadership team
- What to discuss: The objectives are:
  - Team building
  - Reviewing progress
  - Financials and company performance
  - Reviewing the marketplace and competition
  - Reviewing and updating the strategy & talent plan
  - Resetting goals, goal priorities, and ActON plans for the next sprint.
- When to have it: At the end of each sprint. Your organization will decide whether its sprints will be three or four months.
- Where to have it: Off-site. There's something more effective about working on a business when you're

off-site; the physical distance can enhance the perspective that's ideal for these meetings, keeping you clear of day-to-day workplace distractions.
- How long it lasts: The recommended duration is six hours, concluding with a team event and/or dinner.

5. Company meeting

Either virtual or in person, this meeting is essential to excelling at execution, as it engages and energizes all team members in working on the business. This interactive event is held after the sprint meeting, providing clarity on how well we executed in the last sprint and, more importantly, on the goals and priorities for the next sprint. Clarity across the organization leads to better execution of your strategy & talent plan. Everyone makes better decisions when they know where they're going, why, and how.

- Who owns it: The company leader
- Who attends: All team members
- What to discuss: The objectives are:
  - Team building
  - Reviewing company performance and progress since the last sprint
  - Reviewing company goals for the next sprint
  - Engaging all employees in department plans
  - Communicating any announcements.
- When to have it: Within two weeks after each sprint meeting so departments can update their department plans to focus on the goals for the next sprint.

- Where to have it: In a conference room, and/or via videoconference
- How long it lasts: The recommended duration is between 30-60 minutes

6. 1:1 meeting

This is a meeting between the team member and his or her leader to ensure effective communication and connection, and to further team members' development while reviewing their individual talent plan.

- Who owns it: Any leader in the organization with direct reports
- Who attends: Either the company leader and a leadership team member, or a department leader and a department team member
- What to discuss: Anything and everything. The leader and team member should agree on what is most important to discuss. For example,
  - If you want to enhance your relationship, use the start, stop continue exercise. (See Talent Planning toolkit in Chapter 12 for more information.)
  - Update team member's action plans for his or her development.
  - If you need to more effectively communicate, review the dos and don'ts of communication from their DISC behavioral science assessments.
- When to have it: Once a month

- Where to have it: Both attendees should decide together on the location.
- How long it lasts: The recommended duration is 60 minutes.

7. Huddle meeting (optional)

These quick meetings are a great way to communicate foreseeable issues for a given day—particularly if someone needs help completing priorities.

- Who owns it: Any leader in the organization with direct reports
- Who attends: Leader and direct reports
- What to discuss: The objectives are to communicate any check-ins and updates, and to establish individual priorities for the day (or until the next huddle, depending on your chosen cadence). Does anyone need help completing his or her priorities?
- When to have it: Some companies have a huddle every morning, others have one every other day. At my organization, we hold huddles on Mondays and Wednesdays. Other companies will find this extra meeting to be overkill, and that's fine, too—this is all about establishing the best, most effective cadence for your organization.
- Where to have it: In a conference room, and/or via videoconference
- How long it lasts: The recommended duration is 10-15 minutes, with two minutes devoted to

each person to individually run through the suggested agenda.

Stick to It

Among the most common complaints that new clients share with me is the stark truth that communication is utterly ineffective at their organization—that their meetings are even worse than just being a waste of time, with the lack of focus demoralizing and alienating team members who genuinely want to make progress.

Evaluate the meetings you currently have, and if they're ineffective, irregularly scheduled, or inefficient, implement a meeting cadence. Like so many of the other components of the Talent Planning process, a version of the meeting cadence can be implemented as a standalone initiative.

A meeting cadence is, however, incredibly effective at turning a strategy & talent plan into reality. At EnzoPac we kept our cadence for over five years. Our sales jumped from 5 million to 8 million in our first year, and 8 to 15 million in our second year, ultimately growing from 5 million to 30 million over that five-year span. I fully credit our meeting cadence for delivering our strategy & talent plan and achieving (a much celebrated) victory. We were able to get so much done, so much more quickly because we stuck to our cadence.

A meeting cadence instills a full-on mindset and cultural shift. Not only will your cadence create a culture of consistent and efficient communication, it will also encourage self-discipline and accountability. The openness this facilitates will reduce conflict within your organization, which will be well appreciated by the many people whose natural behavioral styles prefer to avoid confrontation.

Finally, a meeting cadence will also create a culture of winning and excelling. When you're accomplishing all the goals you agreed to take on as an organization, your weeks will consist of regular victories and stacked successes. These victories inform a greater, deeper sense of victory and purpose, and create the kind of winning culture to lead to your ultimate victory: achieving your three-year vision.

10

Shepherd of the Talent

"The growth and development of people is the highest calling of leadership."
— Harvey S. Firestone

There you have it! You're now thoroughly versed in the seven steps of Talent Planning. I've spent over twenty years fine-tuning this process, basing it not only on personal experience—which certainly includes some wisdom gained from making mistakes—but also from developing best practices, honed while advising thousands of companies on their strategy & talent plans. I sincerely hope this process will help you avoid the naïve, time-wasting errors I had to overcome, and that the Talent Planning process will pave the way for your greatest fortunes, monetary and otherwise.

Up to this point, I have largely made the case for Talent Planning by appealing to the financial success your organization will achieve from adopting the process. I speak a lot about growing your people and growing your business, but now I want to especially focus on growing your people regardless of your business. As you become a talent planner, I want to talk about embracing your role as a shepherd of talent.

In fact, I want you to see this more as a responsibility than a role.

Your Solemn Duty

Webster's Dictionary defines a shepherd as "a person who protects, guides, or watches over a person or a group of people."

Isn't that what we do every day, whether running a business, a department, or a family?

The ability to develop others, whether at work or at home, is the most important skill of any leader. To own and embrace this approach to leadership is to be a shepherd of the talent.

A shepherd of the talent nurtures, cares for, develops, and holds accountable the talent they are responsible for. Every organization (and every home) needs a shepherd of the talent, resulting in high-performance teams and healthy families. One of the greatest rewards for leaders is to invest in the people in their life, and to witness these people go on to experience success. Candidly, it's addicting; it feels so good when people come back years later and thank you for this. It confirms you've upheld your duty.

Especially for parents, being the shepherd of the talent for your children is a no-brainer; it's pure intuition to help your kids develop and thrive, to empower them, and to aid their efforts as they find their way through their lives and careers. Personally, embracing this role for my now-grown kids—all four of whom have found terrific success living out their passions in their lives and their careers—has been one of the greatest and most rewarding experiences of my life.

For a business leader, though, taking such responsibility for his or her direct reports may not be an automatic or instinctual concept. Yet, there are profound direct and indirect results leaders experience from shifting to this mindset and shepherding our team members.

Short- and Long-Term Benefits

Being a shepherd of the talent is yet another approach to being proactive about people issues.

Why should a job seeker choose to work for your company instead of your competitors? Why should a talented individual stay on your team, rather than take a chance elsewhere?

When your company develops a reputation for developing its team members—for caring about them and their future—you will not only develop an employer-of-choice reputation that attracts new talent, but you will retain the talent already on your team by providing them all they need to thrive personally and professionally.

Workplace culture has never been more important than it is today. But for some employers, that may just mean posting our company values or holding a Christmas party. That lack of genuine investment just will not cut it—not in a market that favors jobseekers, or when workers are resigning in great numbers. And when work and communication are increasingly being done remotely or virtually, you'll need to adjust your efforts to establish or maintain connection with team members, or they'll simply check out and seek more fulfilling opportunities.

As a shepherd of the talent, you make it abundantly clear to your team members that you care about them as a total person, and you're invested in their success—even if that means finding success at a different organization. Yes, when you meet with someone and discuss their career goals and passions, the only approach is to be honest about whether your company is a good fit for their current position, career field, or even at your company. If you're shepherding a talented person whose goals can't be fulfilled at your company, think through your connections—perhaps you know the perfect place for this person, and can help them explore this path.

This was evident at a recent team development session when the company leader told his leadership team that he wants them to be passionate about their roles. He got up in front of the room and said, "If you can't find it here, we want to help you figure it out while you're here". As I looked around the room, I could tell that this team was rallying around the leader and was ready to perform at an entirely new level.

The loyalty you'll build with your team by being a shepherd of the talent will have them ready to run through walls for you. Strengthening these relationships, and working to get everyone aligned in a natural, rewarding position, will get your organization excited and firing on all cylinders. Everyone will be grateful for shepherding, including those who, with your guidance, decide to exit the company in pursuit of the dream you've helped them define.

Not only will the attitude within your company be overwhelmingly positive, but the external attitude about your company will be just as favorable. People in communities absolutely talk about conditions and culture at area businesses. Word not only quickly spreads mouth-to-mouth, but even more widely via websites soliciting current and former employees to rank companies, such as Glassdoor and Indeed.

With the company culture and reputation you'll create as a shepherd of the talent, you won't have the people issues experienced at other companies, and people will know it. I've had the immense pleasure of training hundreds of shepherds, and when their businesses advertise a new job, these positions draw stacks of applications and resumes. A shepherd of the talent virtually never experiences employee shortages.

Further, hiring processes improve with this mindset; a shepherd of the talent is incredibly adept at finding the right people for the right roles.

As companies grow, the leader of the company trains various direct reports in the shepherding mindset, and before you know it, a company is full of well-qualified shepherds guiding and caring for talent throughout the organization. Perhaps the only thing better than being a great leader is creating the legacy of developing great leaders.

Becoming a Shepherd of Talent

Credibility is, above all, the requisite factor to becoming a good shepherd of the talent.

In a sense, you'll need to "shepherd yourself" before you can shepherd others. This starts with developing an honest knowledge of yourself, and understanding your natural behavioral style. Becoming aware of and understanding one's own natural style—including strengths and blind spots—must happen in order for a person to own and accept that style and learn how they can then leverage their style to deliver it naturally and successfully. Every shepherd must first understand, own, and leverage their natural style before they can help someone else do the same.

As a shepherd of the talent, you will further your credibility in your 1:1 meetings with your direct reports by coming in HOT, and by sharing your own story first. You'll set the tone for this private conversation by telling as many details of your personal and professional journeys as you're comfortable sharing, knowing your direct report will reciprocate this level of trust. Vulnerably putting yourself out there will show your direct report that you're sincere and humble in a way they could never have understood before. Showing your total self is the only way to establish total credibility.

Your direct report will believe in your desire to shepherd them, with only their best interests in mind, and the ensuing discussions will lead to incredible breakthroughs: "I never recognized how important it was for me to _____," or, "I had no idea _____ was impacting my actions and decisions that way," or, "So *that's* why I've always struggled with _____."

Again, you're doing this out of a responsibility and duty to these people. Their gratitude for these breakthroughs will be off the charts, but you'll need to remind them that this was their discovery—their victory. You may have helped someone recognize they were lost in the wilderness, and helped them see a way out, but ultimately, it was that individual who willed their way out.

As a shepherd of the talent, you do this because you're supposed to. But the people you help will never forget the positive impact you've had on their lives and careers. You don't shepherd people to be rewarded, but the rewards of the loyalty and reputation you've built up are ultimately ten-fold what you put in.

Your Leadership Potential

If the concept of being a shepherd of talent is new to you, I suggest you give it a shot by starting with just one person. Pick any single person at work, and start investing your time and energy into them. Identify the two or three development priorities that will make the biggest positive impact in their life. Try this out, and I guarantee you'll feel so rewarded for

SHEPHERD OF THE TALENT

your effort that you'll only want to do this for more and more people. I bet you can already think of who that first person will be.

I recently asked a leader I'd trained for an update on how things had been going since he'd made the mindset shift and embraced his responsibility as a shepherd. He replied:

"Being the shepherd of the talent has brought a deeper level of connectivity, trust, and transparency to our organization. And it's never been more apparent as we navigate through unique challenges that require teams to stay connected, trust, and care for one another."

Becoming the shepherd of the talent will not only change your organization inside and out, but it will change you, and make you the brilliant, legendary leader you're capable of becoming.

11

Develop and Dominate

"Every problem is an opportunity in disguise."
—John Adams

You didn't need another book or consultant to list all the employment, supply chain, and economic problems out there.

You needed a plan: a strategy & talent plan.

It's what all of us business leaders have always needed. Some of us may have lucked into success in the past without a great deal of planning. Some of us may have had our talent shortages overshadowed by short-term successes. But the employment landscape of the past is unrecognizable today.

We're facing unprecedented job openings, evolving values and motivations, and what generally amounts to an overdriven version of the uncertainty we've always faced as business owners and leaders.

Talent Planning is how we'll prevail.

By developing ourselves, our team members, and our businesses with a strategy & talent plan, we are primed to dominate our industries.

TALENT PLANNING

May the concepts covered in this book take your business into grand, unprecedented prosperity!

You can accomplish successful Talent Planning on your own using this book as your manual—or you can make the process even easier with the MyTalentPlanner software. This highly efficient, scalable software houses every aspect of the Talent Planning process for your organization all in one, remotely accessible place, saving you time. MyTalentPlanner is the all-encompassing tool to help your business enhance accountability, develop leaders, improve execution, and achieve your vision.

Visit **MyTalentPlanner.com** to try the software for free, or to contact a certified Talent Planning advisor today.

The Toolkit

Whether you're doing the heavy lifting of constructing your first talent plan, or you're in the midst of one, tweaking it, and maintaining momentum, this chapter loads you up with all the tools to help you create, improve, and execute your talent plan.

The previous chapter provided the ideal mindset for successful Talent Planning. Here you'll gain full access to the Talent Planning toolkit, containing every resource imaginable to enhance, update, and achieve your strategy & talent plan, and to make you a proficient shepherd of the talent.

The Tools

This kit is stocked with all the tools, resources, and strategic processes to make sure you're getting the most out of the Talent Planning process. Best of all, this toolkit enables you to complete the process on your own, or along with a trained talent planning advisor.

The Talent Planning toolkit is organized into several categories: tools to help strengthen your strategy; tools and trainings to help develop your organization's talent; and books as advanced resources for expertly executing the Talent Planning process.

Dive in a little deeper by picking one of these tools, and you'll likely find the specialized resource so rewarding that you'll want to utilize others. With this toolkit, there is nothing in your way to becoming a great leader.

Strategy

- ▶ Pre-planning questionnaire
    - The pre-planning questionnaire is optional, but is often used to collect content ahead of the Talent Planning process to make the sessions more efficient.
- ▶ Competence hierarchy
    - A visual template to communicate the competence and target markets of your organization.
- ▶ Mission statement
    - An effective communication tool for mission-driven organizations.
- ▶ Competitive competence analysis
    - The competitive competence analysis compares your newly defined competence in your strategic vision to the competence of your top competitors.
    - When you deliver your competence, will it differentiate you from your competitors?
    - Create action plans to strengthen your competence and increase differentiation versus your competitors.
- ▶ Brand strategy
    - Your brand is your number one salesperson. After all, more people will see your brand than your sales team.

THE TOOLKIT

- Your brand consists of your name, logo, and slogan.
- It needs to clearly communicate your competence and/or the benefits of your competence to your target markets.
- Simply put, your brand communicates what you do better than anyone else and why a customer should choose your company over a competitor.

Talent

▶ Behavioral science assessments

- There are six behavioral sciences you can use in executing your talent plan.
- When facing a talent decision, you'll need the right behavioral science and the right process to make the most informed decision.
- Remember that behavioral science assessments do not make the talent decision for you, but they are useful tools to help you make the most informed decision.

▶ Behavioral science training

- Getting trained or certified in the behavioral sciences enables you to effectively execute the talent plan on your own.
- Reach out to your talent planning advisor for information on behavioral science training and shepherd of the talent training programs.

▶ Hiring process

- To ensure you make the right hire the first time, follow these high-level components to the hiring process:

- Define what an optimum performer looks like by creating a job benchmark.
- Build your candidate pool.
- Conduct your first interviews focusing on their hard skills—their technical ability to do the job. Rank them in order of greatest fit for the position.
- Conduct behavioral science assessments with the top two to four candidates.
- Complete a second round of interviews, customized for each candidates' experience and behavioral science results. Use our customized interview question library to develop your questions. Rank the candidates based on their hard skills, and the second interview.
- Make an offer to the candidate with the greatest fit to the position and benchmark.
- Onboard and create his or her first development plan based on the results from the hiring process.

▶ Customized interview question library
- Identify the top three or four skillset gaps for a candidate, and select questions from this library to address each gap.

▶ Team development exercise
- Complete a team development exercise to create a high-performance team that comes in HOT (honest, open, transparent).

▶ Start, stop, & continue exercise
- An incredibly effective process to improve relationships, resolve conflict, and complete performance plans.

THE TOOLKIT

- ▶ Leadership development planning
  - A simple but effective process identifying the top development priorities that will have the greatest impact on a person's professional and personal life.
- ▶ Succession planning
  - Defines what an optimum performer looks like in a given position, based on designated performance benchmarks. Develop internal successors aimed toward these benchmarks to prepare them for the position.
- ▶ Career planning
  - A simple process that defines the optimal career path for a person, at the intersection of the strengths of his or her natural behavioral style and the passions in his or her life.
- ▶ Life mapping
  - A one-page plan that defines the vision for your life, the long-term objectives and the short-term action plans needed to make it a reality.
- ▶ Sales team behavioral science training
  - Train your sales team on how to determine the DISC behavioral style of a customer, so they can adapt their style in the moment for a successful sales call.
- ▶ 360 performance review
  - This review provides feedback from an individual's leader, direct reports, and peers based on their performance in five leadership categories, and how they can improve.
- ▶ Employee/organizational surveys
  - To ensure you are achieving your desired culture, all employees are invited to complete an anonymous survey to provide feedback.

- Many companies repeat this process every two or three years to measure their progress against their vision.

Books

▶ Stop Selling Vanilla Ice Cream

- This book will help answer the most important strategic question for your business: "Why will a customer choose to do business with you versus your competitors, and pay you more for it?"

▶ Stop the Vanilla in Your Career and Life

- This book contains a simple four step process to help you find your optimum career–at the intersection of your passions and natural strengths. The book also includes the life mapping process to create your one-page life plan.

Toolkit Tips

- Countless leaders have transformed their team and organization by using the Talent Planning toolkit to execute their talent plan.
- To get started with behavioral assessments, start with using one science and one process at a time.
- When using the toolkit for hiring, first, make a great hire. Second, put a development plan in place for each team member. This will dramatically

reduce the ramp-up time for the new team member and increase the ROI of the new hire.

- Training other leaders across the organization on these tools will accelerate the success and growth of your organization ten-fold.

Appendix

Now that you've read chapter 9 of this book, you may want to dive deeper into the methodology of your meeting cadence. This appendix provides detailed agenda suggestions for all seven meetings recommended for the Talent Planning process, as well as tips specific to each meeting.

Leadership meeting
Suggested agenda:

1. Total person updates (10 minutes)
   - To reconnect as a team, go around the room. Each person updates the team on happenings in their professional and personal life.
2. Review ActIN plans (5 minutes)
   - Review the ActIN plans from the last meeting to ensure accountability.
3. Review your updated financial vision (5 minutes)
   - Review all the metrics to ensure our plan is working.
   - Discuss any metrics that are not on track and develop ActON and/or ActIN plans to improve the metric.

4. Company strategic decisions (10 minutes)
   - Discuss any strategic decision/challenges that need to be discussed by the leadership team.
   - Establish priorities for the week.
5. Department/customer updates (15 minutes)
   - Each leader will discuss any department updates they have and share any wins and successes from their department.
   - Resolve any customer issues.
   - Establish weekly priorities by department.
6. Review any issues/opps list (30 minutes)
   - All team members recommend items that should be added to the agenda, then prioritize and resolve them as time allows.
7. Discuss outbound communication (5 minutes)
   - What are the top two or three priorities that need to be communicated to the rest of the organization via department meetings?
8. Review the ActIN plans (5 minutes)
   - Review the ActIN plans that resulted from the meeting and assign an owner and due date.
9. Closing remarks (5 minutes)
   - Go around the room, with each person providing one positive comment and one improvement for the meeting.

Meeting tips:

- Designate a team member to document the meeting results.
- Leader: be ready to share the updated financial vision and any strategy or talent updates.
- Leadership team members: come prepared with your department or customer updates and comments regarding the week ahead.
- This agenda is built on our best practices, but by all means, customize it to fit your needs.

Plan execution meeting

Suggested agenda:

1. Opening remarks (5 minutes)
   - Given by the leader.
2. Reviewing financial statements versus budget (10 minutes)
3. Review financial vision (5 minutes)
   - Ensures the plan is working.
   - Review all the metrics.
   - Discuss any metrics that are low and develop ActON or ActIN plans in order to improve the metric.
4. Review company goals (5 minutes)
   - Review the progress on company goals and develop any ActON or ActIN plans to improve the performance of any goals that are not on track.

TALENT PLANNING

5. Review any ActON plans that are due (25 minutes)

- The owner of the ActON plan reviews the results of completing the ActOn plan.
- The team decides if a given ActON plan is completed. If not completed to the team's satisfaction, set a new due date.

6. Review financial vision for each department (15 minutes)

- This ensures whether a given department plan is working.
- Review all related metrics.
- Discuss any metrics that are not on track and develop ActON or ActIN Plans to improve the metric.

7. Strategy and talent vision updates/adjustments (10 minutes)

- Based on the results of the plan execution meeting, discuss and document any beneficial adjustments to your strategy and talent plan.

8. Closing remarks (5 minutes)

- Go around the room, with each person providing one positive comment and one improvement for the meeting.

Meeting tips:

- Ensure the leader and department leaders are ready to share their financial vision.

- If someone misses a due date once or twice, discuss why, and reset the due date. However, if a team member consistently misses due dates, that must be addressed privately by the leader.
- Designate a team member to document the meeting results.
- This agenda is built on our best practices, but by all means, customize it to fit your needs.

Department meeting

Suggested agenda:

1. Total person updates (10 minutes)
2. Review ActIN plans from previous meeting (5 minutes)
3. Review company updates and announcements (5 minutes)
4. Review department's financial vision (5 minutes)
   - If there are any low metrics, develop ActON plans for improvement.
5. Review sprint goals and ActON plans (15 minutes)
6. Review ay issues/Opps list (30 minutes)
   - All team members recommend items that should be added to the agenda, then prioritize them as time allows.
7. Review ActIN Plans from meeting (5 minutes)
8. Closing remarks (5 minutes)

- Go around the room, with each person providing one positive comment and one improvement for the meeting.

Sprint meeting
Suggested agenda:

1. Opening remarks (5 minutes)
   - The leader sets the stage for the day.
2. Team development exercise (60 minutes)
   - There are several options you can use for a team development exercise:
     - Complete an abbreviated version of the team development session you did in Step 2 of theTalent Planning process.
     - Have a productive conversatioin about the makeup of the team and how they can perform better.
     - Review the "dos and don'ts" of communication for each person
     - Choose a team development exercise of your choice.
   - The key objective is to make sure the team comes in HOT (Honest, Open, Transparent).
3. Review financial statements versus budget (15 minutes)
4. Competitive competence review (30 minutes)

APPENDIX

5. Review and update strategic vision and financial vision (30 minutes)

    - How are you progressing toward achieving your vision?

6. Review and update your talent vision (30 minutes)

    - Discuss any changes that would improve the three-year future functional structure and talent vision.

7. Review department plans (50 minutes)

    - Each department takes 5-10 minutes to review their:
        - Financial vision
        - Current structure
        - Talent plan
        - Completion of their ActON plans

8. Review company talent plan (20 Minutes)

    - Are there any changes we need to make to our leadership team or department talent plans?

9. Reset company goals for next sprint (35 minutes)

    - Elect a goal champion
        - A goal champion is usually a leadership team member that takes ownership of ensuring all the ActON plans necessary to achieve the goal are in the plan and executed.

10. Define ActON plans to achieve each goal (90 minutes)

TALENT PLANNING

- Each ActON plan needs an owner and due date.
  - I recommend splitting the leadership team into brainstorming teams for 15 minutes before regrouping, to facilitate more input.
  - Review your "parking lot" for ActON plans.

11. Next steps to finalize goals and ActON plans (10 minutes)

    - Schedule company meeting to communicate progress from last sprint and goals for next sprint.
    - Department leaders update their department plans with a specific focus on the ActON plans their department is going to complete to achieve the company's goals.
    - Leader and goal champion collaborate to ensure the ActON plans to achieve each goal are documented.

12. Closing remarks and around the horn (15 minutes)

    - Go around the room, with each person providing one positive comment and one improvement for the meeting.

13. Host a team event/meal

Meeting tips:

- Designate a team member to document the meeting results and updates.

- Update your sprints every three or four months to keep your process agile and enable your team to evaluate your strategy and talent plan, modifying it as needed.

- I strongly recommend that the sprint meetings are held offsite, so the leadership team can focus on strategic thinking without being pulled into their tactical responsibilities.

- Finish the day by celebrating with a team social event.

Company meeting

Suggested agenda:

1. Opening remarks (5 minutes)
2. Review company performance (15 minutes)
    - Evaluate the strategic and financial visions
3. Review current organizational structure (5 minutes)
4. Review company goals for next sprint (10 minutes)
5. Announcements/recognitions (10 minutes)
6. Q & A session (15 minutes)
7. Closing remarks (5 minutes)
8. Celebration/social event

Meeting tips:

- Be sure to include all team members, even if you need to have more than one meeting or at another location.

TALENT PLANNING

- The company presentation engages all team members in the planning process so that you accelerate growth by having more people working on the business.

- As you consistently communicate where the company is going, team members will increasingly provide great ideas to achieve those goals.

One-on-one meeting

Suggested agenda:

1. Total person updates (10 minutes)
2. Review ActIN plans from previous meeting (5 minutes)
3. Review team member's individual talent plan (30 minutes)
4. Review the issues/opps list (5 minutes)
5. Finalize new ActIN Plans (5 minutes)
6. Closing remarks (5 minutes)

Meeting tips:

- These meetings are essential to Talent Planning, assuring proactive conversations to resolve any people issues upstream before they might impact the business.

- Avoid postponing one-on-ones; keep them on your calendar.

APPENDIX

- If you want vulnerability and transparency, you need to show it. As the leader, be vulnerable and share how you are doing and discuss your struggles.

Huddle meeting
Suggested agenda:

1. Daily update
2. Review yesterday's top priority (or, if you're not holding daily huddles, the most recent top priority)
3. Today's top priority (or between today and the next huddle)
4. ActIN/ActON plans that are due
5. Any help needed

Meeting Tips:

- One of the keys to an effective huddle is to come prepared with your priorities defined.
- Stick to a limit of two minutes per person.
- Several leaders have told me their initial reaction was that having a huddle every day would be too much, but once they started holding them, they didn't want to stop.
- Set the huddle meetings for what works best for your organization.

Acknowledgements

To our clients, thank you for your trust, wisdom, and friendship as we fine-tuned the Talent Planning process to grow your people and your organizations. Your drive to proactively create a people first culture and invest in the total person was the inspiration that made all of this happen.

My foundation is my faith and family. Thank you to my parents, Don and Mary Jane, for building a tightly knit family, which includes my sisters, Mary and Diane, and my brothers, Paul, Dave, and Andy.

Matt Day, you are a brilliant and gifted writer. I will always remember the many laughs we had working together to create this content-rich book that is an easy read.

To my business partners, your belief in the vision and in me inspires me every day to make it a reality. Business partners for a while, but friends for life.

To our team, the experience over the last 3 years has been one the most demanding but rewarding processes in my career. And without you, it would not have been possible. A special thank you to Cindy, for your unwavering dedication and support—you are classic. And to Alex for your calm and thoughtful wisdom.

To my four kids—Brittany, Mitchel, Brooke, and Mackenzie—the genuine people you have become and the professional and personal success you have and will achieve is one of my greatest rewards. I am so, so proud of each of you. I love each of you dearly.

Lisa, you have supported me for 30-plus years and have made many sacrifices for our family and enabled me to pursue my passion. Can't wait to spend the next 30 years with you, my best friend. All my love to you.

And to Walter and Theo, our wiener dogs, thanks for always making me laugh.

About the Author

Steve Van Remortel is an award-winning author, speaker, advisor, entrepreneur, Saas Software Founder, investor, and recognized thought leader in Strategy and Talent Planning. He founded Stop the Vanilla, LLC in 1999 and has since created a library of 100+ strategy and talent planning methodologies. In 2012, Steve authored his first book *Stop Selling Vanilla Ice Cream: Start Increasing Profits with the Right Strategy & Right Talent*. In 2020, he published his 2nd Book *Stop the Vanilla in Your Career & Life: Love What You Do to Live the Life You Want!*

Steve is founder and CEO of MyTalentPlanner, Inc., a software that enables SMBs to execute talent planning to solve their people issues. He is also Chief Strategist & Talent Advisor at Stop the Vanilla, LLC. He has trained thousands of leaders how to master the skill of talent planning to proactively resolve their people issues and accelerate the growth of their company.

Prior to founding Stop the Vanilla, LLC, Steve led a manufacturing company from $4.5 million to $30 million in sales in five years by having the right plan and the right talent'. He earned his Master's in Strategic Management after a BA in Marketing and Organizational Communications. Steve is a Certified Professional Behavioral Analyst (CPBA) in four behavioral sciences.

Steve and his wife Lisa, raised their four children in Green Bay, Wisconsin, where he was named Businessperson of the Year. Connect with Steve at any of the following:

stopthevanilla   stevevanremortel   myTalentPlanner

ııı TalentPlanner
ACCELERATE GROWTH ®

The only operating system that helps you dominate your industry with the right *people & strategy*.

Key Features

Strategy, Talent, & Execution All in One
Only operating system for SMBs that ties your talent plan/decisions to your strategy.

Win at Strategic HR
Talent Plans at every level of the organization that develop the total person.

Dominate Your Industry
Outperform your competition by working on the business to achieve your goals by executing your action plans.

Better Execution
Consistent and focused meetings lead to better communication, transparency, accountability and execution of your plan.

Try MyTalentPlanner Operating System for FREE! Visit

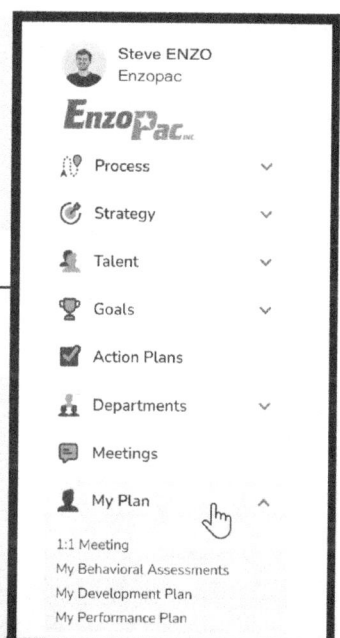

Steve ENZO
Enzopac

Enzopac

- Process
- Strategy
- Talent
- Goals
- Action Plans
- Departments
- Meetings
- My Plan
  - 1:1 Meeting
  - My Behavioral Assessments
  - My Development Plan
  - My Performance Plan

www.MyTalentPlanner.com
info@mytalentplanner.com
920.610.0955

Made in the USA
Monee, IL
24 April 2024